IT'S ALL ABOUT THE DECISIONS WE MAKE

SHARAT SRINIVASULA
POORNIMA MYNAMPATI

Cover design by Poornima Mynampati

For everyone who wants to read a book worth reading

CONTENTS

AUTHORS NOTE

Have you ever noticed that adults are the majority of people who read motivational and success books? And by the time they decide to read these books, they either feel that they have failed in their life and are looking for ways to rebound, or they're seeking inspiration and confidence to improve their current lives, or are undergoing a mid-life crisis and searching for an identity. We think instilling inspiration, confidence, and a purpose in life long before said life goes the wrong way will charge individuals in a positive way to achieve more personal success and accomplishments. We also believe that a transformative moment early in life will clarify one's purpose, instills an unshakable belief in self, inspires to set higher goals, and initiates an action plan for achieving those goals with hard work and devotion.

Make no mistake. The scope of this book ranges from very young to very old, and anyone in any stage of life can read, enjoy, and be inspired by this book. However, we believe in the immense influence this story can have on young readers who are still deciding their paths. Hence, we decided to mold the book such that high school- and college-aged population actually want to read.

But it is true that the majority of teenagers or young adults would not prefer to spend their spare time reading a self-help book as they would rather spend time on social media, watching TV, or playing video games. But one thing that all students must do is study for the standardized university entrance tests such as the SAT/ACT and GRE. That said, we ventured to write a story that appeals to those students, and which incorporates common SAT/ACT and GRE vocabulary in the book, so that the teenagers and young adults are able to read this book as part of their preparation for these exams.

Naturally, we asked ourselves, *"Why would someone read this book rather than the plethora of SAT/GRE books available in the market?"* Based on our research, many high school and college level students are preparing for SAT and GRE verbal portions in a rather unproductive manner - forcibly storing the meanings of the words in their brain, but later unable to recall the meaning or use the word in a sentence, let alone understand how the word is used. In our exploration, we found out that words learned in context, or as part of a grand story, enjoy better memory and recall than those learned out of context.

Context-based learning helps to better encode the meaning of a word and is effective at enhancing the recall of the meaning by reminding the context in which the word appeared. In addition to learning in context, scientific research has also shown that other techniques such as attentive repetition, deep learning, and sleeping shortly after acquisition of new material can vastly improve memory and recall. Utilizing this learning technique, in this book, we seamlessly integrated 1200 of the most frequent SAT/GRE words in sentences into a story that's uplifting, motivational, and that drives readers toward a path to success.

We strongly believe that our principles mold our character and our thoughts guide our conduct. Though the characters are fictional, certain parts of the story as well as some events and incidents are inspired from our own personal life experiences. Thus, we classify this book as "realistic fiction", which we hope is motivational and educational, and helps people take that first step in the right direction with correct principles and values to empower their minds to turn their lives around, forge a stronger self to improve the quality of their current lives, and inspire to build a better life while not being discouraged by transient failures.

An idle brain is considered a devil's workshop. Though an idle brain is perilous, we also understand that even more dangerous and several fold worse than being idle is reading a bad book. As we firmly believe that the greatness of a book is gauged by the degree to which it improved the reader's life, we made every effort to make this book not only interesting and amusing, but also illuminating, inspiring, instructive, and as a valuable learning experience in developing one's character. In this earnest effort, we touched several topics ranging from friendships to interview etiquette, betrayal to sacrifice, addictions to redemptions, fears to life changes, and mindsets to making wise decisions.

How to use this book? Whether you are reading this book for education, inspiration, or just as your weekend or vacation novel, we suggest you first browse the meanings of the words listed in the appendix or have a dictionary app ready on your electronic device. This will not only improve your vocabulary, but will also help you better understand the story. If you are reading this book as part of preparation for a standardized test, we suggest you first read the entire book once and highlight any unknown words in the appendix. After you've learned the meanings of the highlighted words, read the book again to test your memory and to permanently imprint the meanings in your brain. We encourage you to read this book over and over again to reinforce words that you already know, and to continue to learn new words until you get all the words etched in your memory for your personal recall and/or use.

We believe that the greatest gift that one can give to another is a good book. We've received several children books from our friends, and every time we read them to our kids, we remind the person who gave us that fantastic book. If you believe this book will change the life of a teenager or college student, please suggest this book to them. The receiver will remind you every time they read, or when they suggest the book to someone else. And as the giver, you will always be remembered.

We wrote this story to enhance people to live lives to their fullest potential. We wrote to provide thought-provoking inspiration and to propel readers to identify a purpose in life. We strongly believe that justifying our existence with well-intended goal and work that outlasts the humanity is what makes us 'human'.

With wings, everyone can fly. We hope this book gives you wings.

Sharat Srinivasula
Poornima Mynampati
poornima.sharat.ms@gmail.com

SYMBIOSIS

I woke up startled, with my heart palpitating through my chest. I knew very well that I needed a good night's sleep before my big day, but I couldn't sleep soundly for a couple of reasons. Those reasons were named Laila and Luke. Every night I slept with them right next to me. In fact, I'd never even left them for more than eight hours straight. Every night, we read a bedtime story, enact it, group hug and kiss goodnight. Even with plenty of room on the bed, Luke, my one-year old, loved to wake up in the middle of the night, crawl close, and sleep on top of me. Though he would constrain and physically restrict me moving during the night, frankly, I didn't mind him sleeping on me.

As I lay there in bed that night, calming my heart with steady yoga breaths, the pillow on my chest I used as a substitute did Luke no justice. Even though I knew I set the alarm on my phone and ensured the phone was fully charged, I still spent most of the night tossing, turning, and waking up to make sure 6AM had not come and gone. When I woke this time, I saw that it was 5:44 am. My heart rate finally started to subside.

It was early morning, Friday, December 14, 2029, and I was still in awe that I'd scored an in-person interview from SYMBIOSIS, the Arizona-based private space exploration company accelerating the development of technologies for expanding human presence in space. I had flown into Phoenix from Chicago the previous night, and the beginning of my journey to this meeting had not been without drama.

My dad and I had started early in the afternoon to the airport so he could return home before the forecasted snowstorm began, but I got worried and anxious when his car broke down on our way to airport. After nearly fifteen minutes of futile attempts to restart the antiquated vehicle, my dad instructed me to book a cab out of concern that flights were going to be cancelled because of the snow. Fortunately, I reached the airport on time, but my flight ended up being delayed for about an hour.

When I finally landed in Phoenix, the first thing I noticed was the stark disparity in the weather for which I'd prepared; Phoenix, known for its torrid summers, is absolutely beautiful in winter. It was 70 degrees, bright and sunny, and I took in a pleasant sunset zephyr as I called home to make certain my dad got home safely. Though he did, our family car needed to get towed. I took a rideshare from the airport to the lovely hotel the company had arranged where I had strived to relax my mind and body with a room service dinner followed by a warm bath, enhanced by a cocktail of aromatherapy oils. After some controlled breathing techniques, compliments of my weekly yoga, I attempted to go to sleep early in preparation for my big day.

Because of my fitful night, I tried to sleep for another fifteen minutes. But when I was unsuccessful, I decided to get up and get ready for the interview. I turned on my favorite music, pulled the clothes out of my suitcase and ironed them. Then I took a cold shower, washed my hair, and put on casuals bought specifically for the interview. To test how my outfit and shoes wore, I ran furiously downstairs to the hotel lobby for some healthy breakfast and coffee. Holding steadily, wary and heedful not to spill any of the bitter sweet coffee on my dress, I carefully carried back upstairs, where I could talk with my parents before I had to leave.

Dad was shoveling eighteen inches of white mess off the driveway and mom was about to wake Laila to get her ready for school. Even with their harried morning schedule, they both took the time to stop and encourage me. "We wish you all the very best, honey," my mother said, and dad echoed the sentiment: "All the very best!" The connection with my family and home left me completely relaxed and confident. After my call, I brushed my teeth again to eliminate bad coffee breath and waited.

Around 8:30, I received a message that my car had arrived. It was a newer model, totally redesigned autonomous car that wasn't yet available for the consumer mass market, and I got a little excited. I diligently scanned my iris for recognition and climbed in, and the car started moving towards my pre-programmed destination. It was a fifteen-minute ride from the hotel to the company headquarters, and though the car moved swiftly, the ride was so soft that it felt like the car was traveling at glacial speed.

I pulled my phone out and started to go over my schedule for the day. My first interview was with Human Resources, followed by two group interviews, a brief presentation, and then lunch with one of the vice-presidents of the company. I was scheduled to be done with interviews by 1:30PM. Though I researched the company and all of my interviewers thoroughly on every social media resource that I could find, I was still tense knowing I had only one shot at making a good impression. "I need this job," I said to myself, well under my breath in case the car interior had a camera. My career growth was stunted in my current position, and in addition to working with the latest technology and challenging projects, the major salary increase would mean everything to my family.

The car started to slow down, and I could see a security gate in the distance. I had been emailed that my interview was in Building 11 and I wondered how long it would take me to find it. As the car approached the security gate, a laser scanned the car tag and then my iris. I reached for the car door, expecting it would unlock, but the vehicle continued moving and within a minute stopped in front of Building 11. The door unlocked and opened automatically.

Building 11 was tall and huge; all other adjacent buildings looked diminutive compared to it. The lobby was elegant and as if the theme was 'soft corner', all furniture and surfaces were curved and smooth, including a colossal seamless spherical TV hanging from the ceiling. Except for few others who appeared to also in attendance for interviews, I couldn't find any company staff. As I scanned my iris yet again, I was notified by an automated voice that someone named Amanda would be out in five minutes to greet me. I decided to take that brief opportunity to use the restroom, check my breath, and wash my sweaty palms. As I was walking back towards the front lobby, I noticed the walls. There were no accent walls; instead they depicted the modest origin of the inchoate days and delineated the entire history of the company with all their salient triumphs and fiascos.

The walls didn't have anything new that the company website didn't have. In fact, it was the picture of these walls that was in the company website but seeing them up close was more majestic and persuasive. Usually corporations make it prominent only their grand successes and accomplishments. However, those walls represented the company's record with absolute fidelity. Starting with their first misadventure with asteroid mining, there were more failures pictured than triumphs, but no dead-ends. While the wall on one side of the corridor depicted the advancements in space exploration, the opposite wall showed the same timeline but the benefits from such exploration bestowed to Earth.

There was a general misconception among people that exploring elsewhere is nothing but neglecting Earth, especially when there is still so much work that needs to be done here. But in the limited time I had, I noticed a section of the wall that clearly illustrated how the ultra-lightweight materials **SYMBIOSIS** developed for deep space exploration were now used in medical products for saving human lives, thus educating people the necessity of space exploration is not only for humanity's curiosity of the great beyond and the unknown, but is also advantageous for every being living on Earth. Sections of each wall were separated by fresh green plants and though each section has a story to tell, in the interest of time, I hastily walked towards the building's entrance.

Soon, a lady's voice called my name. "I am Alex," I replied.

Amanda introduced herself, and in a diplomatic tone, informed me she would be coordinating my interviews. I followed her into a meeting room like a docile puppy compliantly traipsing behind its owner.

"Alex," Amanda said, referencing a tablet she swiped confidently, "You will have your HR interview from 9am to 10am. You will then have two group interviews, each lasting about forty minutes, later followed by your presentation. Around 12:30, Vice-President Ann Carol will accompany you for lunch."

Within a minute or so, an HR professional entered the room and introduced himself as Dave. I greeted him warmly, gleaning a bit of satisfaction from his demonstration of excitement to meet me. "Well," Dave began, getting comfortable in his chair, "I'm sure you've read up about us, but let me explain who we are." I nodded, crossing my ankles under the table and leaning forward with clasped hands to look more engaged.

"Our humble beginning ten years ago was initiated by a simple mission to provide efficient systems and robust technologies to explore low-Earth orbits, and for a safe, reliable, and permanent expansion of human presence beyond Earth. In our initial years, we had less than five hundred employees. But after a couple of successful missions to near-Earth orbits and asteroid mining operations, we progressively augmented our demanding targets and also saw an exponential growth in the company. Currently, we are more than 10,000 employees strong. We deal with almost every aspect of space exploration, from reusable launch vehicles and transportation systems; infrastructure and habitation systems; to communications and life support systems. Not an attempt to boast, but we believe we have the best research and development facilities globally, which is bolstered by strong collaborations with universities. I'm sure you're also aware that we provide educational aid to any employee who wants to further their education in whichever field they want to explore, including providing financial aid to needy students."

I nodded my head, showing my appreciation. Dave had not told me anything I didn't know, which he seemed to sense. He smiled an HR smile and said, "So. Tell me about yourself."

I had written several drafts in preparation for that HR's widely revered favorite question. During that time, I asked myself: Why does the interviewer ask such an open-ended question? Are they lethargic? No. They are not lazy because they do spend hours studying the resumes to identify potential candidates. That said, they are definitely not looking for me to recite my resume either. They want to know what *I* consider the highlights and milestones in my career. They want to know me as a person and if I take ownership in my work. And finally, they want to understand my ambitions.

When I interviewed myself, I struggled with whether I should start with my personal details or strictly limit my response to my professional career. I had finally decided to exclude my personal details. As Dave cleared his throat patiently, "I built my career in project management," I said. "With a B.A. in Journalism from Harvard, and an MBA from the University of Chicago, I started working for Fleet, an autonomous vehicle manufacturing company. In my current role as Junior Program Manager, I oversee project goals, requirements, rigorous schedules, requisitions, and resource allocation. I am accountable for handling R&D projects from start to finish."

I went on, adding that though not a part of my job duties, I also provide media specialist and marketing support when needed. I finally concluded that in my quest to expand my skill set, I was looking for new opportunities. "I truly believe that this job is a perfect fit," I concluded confidently.

Dave nodded and quickly followed up with - "Why are you looking for a change?"

I was aware that this was a more perilous question than the previous one, primarily because it was loaded. I could never deduce what the motivation for the question was: Does the interviewer want to know if I have issues with my current employer? Or if I am a risk-taker looking for challenging tasks? Or if I'm motivated by the salary, status and the job profile, or all of the reasons combined? I was expecting this question, but still I struggled with nothing but trite and banal answers rolling around in my mind. I wanted to be careful not to badmouth my current employer and concluded that the best way to crush that question was not to give a hackneyed answer, but instead be original and exploit the basic human propensity.

I leaned forward again. "Modern humans are explorers. Ever since small bands of nomadic humans left Africa several thousands of years ago, we developed the penchant for taking risks and expanding into new territories. As humans are hardwired to explore the unknown, I have decided to push my boundaries and look beyond the horizon. I don't see this job as a career change, but the next step in my career growth path. And based on my earlier phone and video conversations with the technical manager, I understand that I have an immense career growth potential in SYMBIOSIS."

I made sure not to look too satisfied with myself, although I knew I sounded well-prepared. I breezed through several more stock questions about my greatest accomplishment, how I handled working under pressure, and the major challenges and problems I faced in my current job. As Dave quickly typed notes into a tablet, he seemed adequately impressed with my clarity and confidence in my replies.

He looked up after a moment with one brow raised. "Do you have any questions for me?" he asked. I had low expectations of receiving a gratifying answer, but, in a deferential tone, I still proceeded with asking, "Over the years, I have seen so many companies doing mass layoffs, but I have never heard any such thing going on in SYMBIOSIS. What is the reason behind this?"

Though I am adept at reading and decoding emotional and facial expressions, I couldn't read any discernable reaction to my question. Instead, as if expecting it, he replied, "The reason is because of the symbiotic relation we have between employees and the leadership. Everything SYMBIOSIS achieved so far belongs to our employees. Every employee owns a piece of the company. People come here and become employees to make their dreams come true. While the traditional thinking is that employees work for salary, we think that all we do is provide resources to make their dreams and goals a reality, and in that process our employees also make money.

"Our employees don't leave because they love their work and enjoy the challenges. We facilitate this by providing state-of-the-art facilities and cutting-edge tools and technology. We encourage employees to fully contribute in any role they are passionate about, and **SYMBIOSIS** values their opinions authentically. The success belongs to each and every employee, and we make sure that the employees are recognized and appreciated for their contributions.

"However, that isn't enough because passionate people working in a bad company will only produce mediocre results. Hence, just as every employee is accountable for their own actions, we empower every employee with the freedom, voice, and power to hold the leadership accountable. This increases employee's confidence and trust in the leadership, which automatically transfers to better productivity. Our leadership principles are trust and transparency. Because of these principles, we are able to flourish and grow.

"Even so, once any company has streamlined its focus and direction, we also learned that the most common reason a company lays off employees is to cut their costs and boost their profits so that the top management can be paid anywhere between 100 to 400-fold higher than the average salary of an employer. Our CEO's pay is on par with our employees. Our company is founded on the principle that the hunger of the employees and their intellectual appetite makes up the company, and not the other way around. Our leadership has also cultivated a culture of flexibility while providing stability, strength, support and security. We toiled under our leadership to be the benchmark for how the companies should be run, a model for everyone out there on how the companies should take care of their employees. We believe that companies need employees as much as employees need a job. Employee and employer are co-dependent, sharing a common goal. And that is exactly what **SYMBIOSIS** stands for. We believe in interdependent interplay between employer and employee, with advantage to both."

I wasn't expecting such an exceptional reply and found myself even more excited at the prospect of getting the job. It seemed like exactly what I thought it would be - an extraordinary opportunity to work for a world-class, revolutionary company. Many companies make a mistake by treating employees as mere workers as if they are just hired to do a job. The secret for a successful company is to provide safety, give some freedom and let the employee love and respect the workplace. Consequently, the employee will definitely love and be accountable for their work. Employees should look forward to work every day not because they feel insecure about their job but because they love what they do. There is certainly a marked difference in productivity when one works hard as opposed to when one loves to work, because one sees a meaning in their work. And patently, appreciation is a great motivator in all aspects of life.

"Thoughts?" Dave asked, interrupting my actual thought process.

I nodded approvingly that extraordinary achievements do begin with extraordinary workplace culture.

Moments later, as we stood to leave, Dave pointed to me casually, "Alex, I noticed from your resume that you did your Bachelors from 2014-2018. Our founder and CEO, Audrianna, also attended Harvard during those years. Did you by any chance know her?"

I smiled. In fact, I knew Audrianna long before Harvard. I knew her from Chicago, where we attended the same high school. As a matter of fact, I also knew the Chief Technology Officer, Ethan, and the Chief Research Officer, Abigail, who both attended high school with us as well. But I didn't wish to exploit my friendships to get the job. I wanted to achieve the job with my own prowess.

I nodded genially. "Yes. I knew Audrianna quite well," I said simply.

I then moved on to group interviews which were comprised of a wide range of people with diverse backgrounds. The incisive questions felt brutal, but not hostile. Again, I was prepared. I knew that while Dave had been looking to ascertain if I was an adaptable and resilient employee who would listen and have passion to do even the meanest parts of the job, at the group level, companies want employees who can work with others for a common goal and handle disagreements while making a contribution. The group interviews appeared undeniably to be devised to test confidence, character, and response under duress, analogous to a military exercise. But I remained placid, composed, and concise in my replies. Still, I found myself stupefied when one of the engineer interviewers asked me bluntly a scrupulously crafted question, "We are living in times when artificial intelligence and machine learning are highly efficient, cheaper, and have minimal failure rates; why should we still hire a human?"

For a moment I was in a quandary. But I knew instinctively that humans trump computers in many ways, particularly given that artificial intelligence is incapable of feelings and instincts. I took my time, improvised an answer from what I had read over the years, and responded with examples that an engineer working in a space exploration company would easily understand. I assertively replied, "The human brain has an amazing ability for pattern recognition. Pattern-processing capabilities have become highly sophisticated with the evolving human brain. Today's advanced computers have tremendous computing power, but humans are still superior at recognizing patterns. Moreover, the ingenuity and adaptability of humans to evaluate in real-time far exceeds any artificial intelligence. Computers only output information what we program them to, which is limited to our theories and understanding. For example, in astronomy, hot Jupiters with very short orbital periods were considered unreasonable and impossible and were originally missed by the computers in the collected data. However later, we humans found dozens of exoplanets that the supercomputers missed. Another example for the need of human touch was the discovery of the most mysterious star in our galaxy, Tabby's star, which was actually found by humans looking at the same data that the very sophisticated computers of NASA Kepler mission missed."

As I concluded my answer, several of the engineers shared satisfied looks. The group sessions, though a bit enervating, were interesting and felt like an exploration. It was also my moment to show how distinctive and uniquely qualified for the position I was.

My presentation to a group of managers and supervisors, summarizing the work I was doing at Fleet and the challenges I handled, went well without a hiccup and I made sure to recapitulate my accomplishments at the end of the talk in the most compelling way possible, in the hope I could implant in them a feeling that I am not made by a cookie-cutter but rather a singular fit for the position.

After my presentation, Ann Carol accompanied me to lunch as planned. On our way to the café, I noticed a group of people surrounding a notice board with a pithy quote on its head - "*Showing vulnerability is an attribute, not a weakness.*" Ann Carol saw me studying it and smiled. After a moment, she spoke. "At SYMBIOSIS, the leadership exhorts employees to express vulnerability in solving problems and asking for help." She elucidated that the notice boards and forums are where solutions to every SYMBIOSIS success have originated, and where people with different backgrounds and manifold areas of expertise propose ideas and solutions.

The café was completely automated and I couldn't find anyone standing in queues waiting to order food. We selected our choices from the digital menus built into our tables and were informed our orders were on the way. No charge was ever accessed. Ann Carol mentioned that the chefs in the kitchen were robots, supervised by humans. The tables were all close to one another, strategically organized with a minimum of six chairs each, ostensibly to promote socialization amongst staff, according to Ann. It seemed to be working; I saw no one using their phones. As employees chatted, I noticed a vivid spark in their eyes. And when an android brought out the food, I was as adrenalized as a toddler visiting an amusement park for the first time. But I quickly stifled my feverish and frenzied excitement, reminded myself that I was in an interview, and reached a negotiated consensus with my brain.

The time was now about 1PM. I was feeling relief that my poor night's sleep had not yet caught up to me, mixed with excitement over what was unfolding before me. **SYMBIOSIS** was amazing. Dave, Ann, the engineers and managers had all proven I'd be happy here. I was so lost in my thoughts, surveying the café, that I barely noticed the hand on my shoulder and the warmth of a presence next to me. When I finally looked back at Ann, she was looking up towards Ethan.

His face was surprised, as I'd expected it might be. "Alex, what are you doing here?" questioned Ethan.

"Well, she's here for an interview, of course," Ann chuckled, as though he should know. Ethan looked at me quickly, a flash of anger in his eyes, perceptible only to me.

"Of course," he said, and then he asked Ann if I could meet with him after the interview. Ann acquiesced to his request and I saw Ethan disappearing into the hallway.

After a while, as the interview came to an end, Ann Carol escorted me to Ethan's office. Though my interview was unexpectedly prolonged, I didn't mind. His assistant informed us that he was on his way back from a meeting and invited me to wait in Ethan's office. The office was spacious and split into two distinct personalities: half mechanic workshop on one side and half immaculate work space on the other side, with a punctiliously arranged lineup of acclaims and accolades displaying his professional trajectory and accretion to the level of CTO.

I'd first met Ethan when we entered high school back in late 2010. He was an average-looking, bashful teenager with awkward metal braces and glasses so strong his eyes looked doubly magnified. He always dressed simply and sat in the first row in every class. He was painfully quiet around girls. He wasn't into sports. Instead, he loved art, writing plays, and poetry. The Bard of Chicago, as I referred to him then because of his excellent poetry and use of unfathomable figurative speech, was one of the canniest students in class. Our friendship wasn't the most natural, or instant. In fact, it came about in an interesting way. Some girls in our classes would tease him because he was so shy, so much so that once, several of the girls started a challenge to get Ethan to talk to a girl. My reputation as the head of the gang was clearly at stake, and so to cement my popularity by winning the contest, I decided to initiate a friendship with Ethan and slowly start to get close to him. What I discovered, however, was that Ethan was a nice guy with good heart. His genial, helpful nature ultimately caused us to click genuinely, and before long we became so close that whenever I was sad, Ethan knew how to make me laugh. And over time, he also became my dearest confidante.

We shared all of our problems in those days, whether regarding life, money, emotions, or a host of insignificant topics. We never ran out of things to discuss, although the majority of our discussions were more like arguments. From silly quarrels to heated altercations, Ethan and I became known for our acrimonious debates and strident squabbles. As close as we were, we rarely agreed on anything, always on opposite ends of the spectrum, breathing in completely disparate worlds of thinking and living poles apart in opinions. Congruity was not in our books as we hardly reach a concord. Ethan was sensitive, but would not hesitate to fight me to death if he believed my opinion or conviction was immoral or unethical.

Despite the incongruity of our opinions, however, we maintained our close friendship throughout high school and well beyond, until our final day in college in May 2018. I had not seen him since college.

While thinking about Ethan, waiting in his office, a nervousness fell upon me. He seemed angry somehow in the cafeteria, and I wondered just what kind of reception I could expect. Just as I considered that I might need to prepare myself for an argument, he stepped into his office with the biggest congenial smile I had ever seen on his face.

ETHAN

My excitement quickly took over, and while I considered it might not be decorous for the environment, I swept Ethan into a hug. I surprised myself with the sudden wetness of my eyes as I heard myself say, "Oh my God, it's been forever!" Ethan reciprocated by nodding his head, and I noticed he too had tears of joy to accompany the grin on his face.

The moment was so lovely and warm, that I nearly forgot about the potential that Ethan was upset with me. But moments after exchanging warm salutations, it was impossible to forget. The tears dried and the smile disappeared as Ethan slipped behind his desk and went straight to the point I'd been dreading since our encounter in the cafeteria.

"Why didn't you tell me you had an interview here?" he demanded. His tone was upset, but his face looked more disappointed than anything. I met his gaze plainly, the result of a comfort with doing so after many years of constructive confrontation. "Ethan, you should know me better than that. I didn't want to take advantage of friendship in any way to get a job here. I'd rather be certain I was hired on the strength of my own merits." He didn't immediately answer, but I could tell by how his shoulders relaxed that he respected my decision.

"How's Philip?" he asked, looking very interested in the answer. Until that point, I hadn't been completely certain that my discussion with Ethan was not a part of my interview, but this extremely personal question set my mind at ease. There would be no more use for formal language, and the tone of our communication would be colloquial from here on out.

He'd asked about Philip, the very last thing or person I'd rather talk about in the world. I noticed Ethan scanning my hands for my wedding ring, which for a legitimate reason I no longer wore.

"Actually," I started evenly, "I'm divorced. My children and I live with my parents." I could see Ethan's brow raise at the mention of kids, so I continued to assuage any confusion. "My daughter Laila is seven-and-a-half and my son Luke is one." Before Ethan could ask me more about Philip, I told him that it is a long story in a tone that made clear I did not have much more to say on the matter. I concurred with his opinion that two little children are a handful, but I quickly settled his qualms by assuring him that I received plenty of help from my parents.

His visual quest for my wedding jewelry led me to his hand, where I noticed his ring. He didn't miss this, and smiled as he shrugged. "There isn't much to tell about me. I am the same old Ethan. After undergrad, I completed my master's. SYMBIOSIS was established in the first week of December 2019, and I was one of the first employees. The rest is history." I mused. He nodded.

"But," I added, "If I recall correctly, you always said that you wanted to do a Ph.D. and become a professor. Something about teaching and guiding students?" It was my turn to raise my brow.

Ethan sighed audibly. "Sometimes things don't go as planned!" I closed my eyes in full emotional agreement, opening them with a huge smile when Ethan then added that he'd very recently finished his part-time Ph.D.

"There's the Ethan I know!" I exclaimed, pleased to see that all had not changed. He swiveled in his office chair a bit, studying me.

"Well, to be honest, I'm still looking for the Alex I know. What happened to you? You're different. This is not the girl I remember. Do I need to ask you for the code word?"

During our high school years, when phone conversations were unofficially decreed obsolete and antediluvian, and popularized text communications became their replacement, Ethan and I set up a code word to ensure we were in fact who we claimed to be. It was our insurance policy against any of the infantile games teens played then with texting, pretending to be someone other than who they were to learn coveted information or to start petty arguments. Back then, we requested the code word at the start of every text. But we never, ever used the code word in-person and I found it funny he asked me now directly to my face. I was also a bit surprised that he made this inquiry about my

13

comportment so soon, but then again Ethan had never been one to mince words with me. I also knew there was indeed a considerable change in my nature. I didn't blame him for his curiosity, but the question made me tired. Much had changed, more than I was willing to discuss here, in his beautiful office, directly following a high-stakes job interview.

I assured him that I was the same Alex he knew from high school and college. "I started drinking coffee," I offered. "Maybe it elicited the change!"

I could tell that he wasn't completely satisfied by my jocular response, but he let it go as my eyes fell to his ring again, silently petitioning information.

"My wife's name is Sydney; she was a family friend. I don't think you ever met her while we were growing up?" I shook my head. The name didn't ring any bells.

"Right. Well, I only met her once or twice myself during childhood. Her parents knew me. But her family actually moved out of state right as we started high school. Anyhow, we ran into each other again after college, and, long story short, we got married. We're currently expecting our first child next month."

Ethan said this casually, but I could tell he was proud. I clapped my excitement, offering my congratulations with a tickled gasp. "Ethan that's *wonderful!*"

He nodded with a small smile, never one to over-emote. "Sydney will be at the reunion tomorrow. You can meet her then."

In obvious response to my earlier coffee joke, Ethan suggested that we continue our conversation with a cup of cappuccino and I agreed to his offer with a perfunctory nod. As we walked toward the kitchen, Ethan said, "I'm sure you're aware being the thorough researcher you are, but in case you didn't know, Abigail also works here."

"You mean Abi, the Brainiac?" I laughed. "The Chief Research Officer of the Life Sciences Team?"

"The very one," Ethan grinned. "Her office is on the way to the kitchen if you want to stop there first?" On our way to her office, I asked more about Abi's work.

"To thrive beyond Earth, at SYMBIOSIS," Ethan began, seeming to have memorized the answer he now rattled off, "we develop exciting space technologies such as climate-controlled living spaces, lightweight radiation shielding, ultralight weight flexible spacesuits, superlight weight and tough materials such as graphene and carbon nanotubes using nanotechnology, renewable power generation and storage, energy transfer using microwaves, laser propulsion and ion engines, materials and electronics research that can weather wide temperature changes, manufacturing processes in microgravity or in vacuum." I leaned in, now riveted by his words, but he stopped then and shrugged. "But that said, frankly, what Abigail does is completely abstruse and beyond the scope of my cognitive capabilities. I don't even pretend to comprehend her work, but all I know is she's into life support and ecosystems." Good old honest Ethan. I felt comforted by his keen, continued similarity to my high school friend. As we continued to walk, probably realizing that he hadn't said much to answer my actual question, Ethan expounded on his words, adding that Abigail was researching anti-radiation drugs to thwart and restore damage to human tissues induced by long-duration exposure to radiation; air, water and food recycling systems; potable water extraction techniques, creating ecosystems conducive for humans to survive and thrive on other planets; manipulating Hayflick limit; cryonics and vitrification; terraforming; and much more. Except for a very few, I did not understand any of the esoteric technologies and terminology Ethan mentioned, but I kept this to myself. I was certain chatting with Abi about it later would be challenging enough.

Ethan abruptly stopped in front of an office door, where a framed quote was prominently displayed on the door. Even though nothing on the door read "Abigail", I glimpsed at it, chuckled, and said, "Yes, I am sure this is her office. Now what does this mean?"

There was a gleam in his eye as he shook his head in response to my inquiry. "Solve it," he said. When he saw what must have been a daunted look on my face, his expression relaxed into one of assurance. "You'll be able to decipher it before you leave SYMBIOSIS. Promise." I took a picture of it with my phone, comforted by Ethan's vow that if I couldn't decode it, I was invited to come back later and see the translation on the backside of the frame.

I peeked inside Abi's office which was an organized mess. There were piles of books decorating every shelf, huge collections of scientific journals, and what appeared to be scientific papers and articles all over the place. But the mad genius herself was nowhere to be found. Ethan informed me that there was a lab on the other side of the office and that Abi could be in there. He didn't offer to take me there.

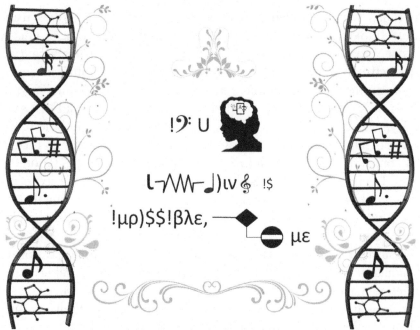

Once we had our cappuccinos and were en route back to Ethan's office, I felt a sadness that I hadn't seen Abi.

"I wish I could have seen Ab-" Before I even finished the sentence, Abi came running out of her office. For a moment, I thought she was running to see me, but it appeared she was just running in general, on her way to somewhere she needed to be. When her eyes fell on me, however, I clocked the surprise on her face. As usual, she left no mystery about her feelings, exclaiming "Alex!" in her jovial tone.

"What a surprise! It's good to see you after such a long time. How have you been? And what are you doing here?" I told Abi that I came in for an interview for a project manager position and that I was also super elated to see her. I adjusted the espresso in my hand and she adjusted the tablet in hers as we exchanged a hug.

Abi politely declined when Ethan asked her to join us, and as it was almost 2PM, I had a pretty good idea why. During college, Abi and Audi, the founder of SYMBIOSIS, always used to have coffee at 2PM, which they called their "Caffeine Kick". Abi and Audi debated intellectually on a wide range of innovative ideas to creative problem solving, pondering which method was best for effective solution and what can be achieved versus what was impossible. Being friends with them both, Ethan and I remained silent and listened during their scholarly disputes, which seemed incessant. But no matter how much they argued and dissented, they never argued during coffee. In fact, Ethan and I used to pray for 2PM so that we could enjoy fifteen minutes of blessed silence. As Abi scurried away, I guessed she was headed to Audi's, for an innocent cup of coffee.

As soon as Ethan and I were back in his office, the encumbrance I had been carrying for many years felt too heavy a weight to bear any longer. I had to finally absolve my heart, recant my statements, and fully reconcile with him. There was, after all, a reason we had not spoken in nearly ten years.

"Ethan, I'm sorry," I blurted out, squeezing my mug as hard as I could to still my shaking hand. He looked up, taken aback.

"Sorry? About what?"

Reluctantly, I evoked his memory of our final altercation during our last days of college, which started as a routine tiff but culminated in ending our friendship. We had bitter strife's before, but never got embroiled in such a fierce conflict.

Ethan and I had very strong and differing opinions regarding money. Ethan believed in earning the hard way, and that money gained in such a way is most satisfying and more highly valued. My stance was that money is money, whether easily gained by luck, or otherwise earned.

Ethan asserted that earning our own money gives a sense of independence and satisfaction that cannot be gleaned from simply winning it. He contended that hard-earned funds build confidence, appreciation, and stability in life, while claiming that one also develops a sense of responsibility. In the course of his cogent arguments, Ethan challenged me most by saying, "Even if I lost my money, I have the confidence to earn it again and again and again because I know how to. But if you lose yours, you cannot repeat your luck."

I was so headstrong in my naive opinions and spurious claims that I obstinately rejected his assertions and vehemently affirmed that I would have the same appreciation for money no matter how I got it. I was indolent and wanted to get wealthy without doing any real work, quickly get rich, and possess everything I ever wanted without any sacrifice. I also preposterously thought I needed money and prestige to be happy and enjoy life.

I could now concede that I was immature and sophomoric to realize that money is simply utilitarian and greed can easily make us a slave. Over the years, I learned that my ludicrous way of thinking to possess and revel in materialistic things obtained without any hard work is indeed hollow, and by no means ingenious like I thought.

Ethan seemed uncomfortable to be traveling down this old road, and I decided to change the subject, content that he was clear that I now realized his wisdom in our younger years. "So," I casually asked, "What about SYMBIOSIS that has made you stick around for such a long time?"

I was uncertain if Ethan's exuberant response was because he was excited to impart his answer or excited that our previous conversation was done. I watched as he uncharacteristically leaned back to rhapsodize. "Well," he started, "you know how much I like stability in life." I nodded with a small concessionary smile, acknowledging his callback to my comments just moments before.

"After my summer internship in 2016, I became fascinated with sensor technology. As a result, I started developing infrared and hyperspectral imaging technology to scan moving asteroids and analyze their composition. After graduation, I immediately enrolled in graduate school; and for my thesis, I developed technology for modular robots to change the orbit of the asteroids and insert them in a trajectory that would corral them into one of the Lagrangian points for mining operations. When I was about to graduate with my master's in December 2019, I decided not to pursue a Ph.D. and instead search for a job to settle down. It was then Audi asked me to come work for her newly established company. I was a novice and had no practical experience as a fresh graduate, but she trusted me so much that she asked me to lead the asteroid mining department.

"As we were pondering on our first project, we all decided to demonstrate the seminal technology I was working on over the years and test it in space. It was an audacious goal and my very first practical project. All the modular robot infrastructure needed was already in space and our task was to use that infrastructure, nudge an M-type asteroid from its orbit, and snare it into one of the gravitationally stable Lagrangian points for later extraction of its ore. I was made the project lead. We selected a small twenty-meter M-type asteroid for this task, which luckily for us was about to swing by close to Earth in about eight months' time. It was actually a very short time frame, but we plotted the course of action, and our team of engineers and mathematicians worked day and night to achieve the task. We were so steadfast and poised that such a bold objective was attainable. We simulated everything, every minute detail, and calculated all the quantitative parameters needed to carry out the task.

"Finally, in August of 2020, the day dawned when we were to actually do it. We were all in the mission control center, very nervous but enthusiastic. We dispatched the robot on a path for the rendezvous with the asteroid. Everything seemed to go well until the very moment we failed to nudge the rock into the right trajectory. Our calculations were wrong. After a perusal examination, we found out that we'd made grievous errors that underestimated some parameters, which resulted in our failure to push the asteroid into the trajectory for stable Lagrangian point. We grossly miscalculated the scale of the entire operation which was much more sophisticated and complex than we thought. My whole team was disheartened, and their confidence was marred by the failure. It was an unprecedented exercise by anyone to prepare an asteroid for mining, and the whole world was looking at SYMBIOSIS. And we failed. As project lead, I let my team and the company down."

Although this was an old story, it still brought Ethan down. He continued, as though he heard my thoughts. "I just sunk down in my chair, despondent and depressed," Ethan muttered under his breath. "Audi saw me, lying morose and dead in my chair, and approached me. I'm sure you remember how little Audi speaks. But when she does, it's always uplifting. Without a twinge of disappointment in her tone, she simply said to me, 'Ethan, don't be discouraged. This is our very first attempt at a formidable task. Do you remember the very first day you started to learn to ride a bicycle without training wheels? You probably thought you were ready without the training wheels, but I'm sure you fell down several times. Falling off is awkward and unpleasant, but you were willing to go through that to become proficient over time. Sometimes, regardless of how prepared and calculated we are, we fail. It is awkward, embarrassing, and disappointing. But just like we go back and keep trying to ride the bike, we should keep going and try again and again until we succeed at whatever we do. Mistakes and failures are just opportunities for learning something new. As the leader of your team, you should not be scared of failure. Start asking the right questions because questions drive the results. Concentrate on the positives that came out of this failed endeavor and focus on attempting again. And don't worry about the press conference. I will handle it.'

"At the press conference later that day, Audi told reporters that she failed. Usually, when something goes wrong, people in the leadership try to blame someone for the disaster and try to shift the responsibility for the loss. But, Audi, the CEO of the company, took my failure and made it her failure. She voluntarily made herself a scapegoat.

"After Audi's inspiring words and stunning display of leadership, my team regained our lost confidence and courage. Her words were so supportive that everyone on the team felt that we could achieve our objectives, goals, and dreams. By remaining sanguine and of pertinacious spirit, we quickly got back on track and started questioning our assumptions. Within six months, in February of 2021, we attempted again... and this time we succeeded. Our whole team was jubilant. This time, Audi asked me to go take the press conference and told me to announce to the world that my team succeeded in achieving this arduous and formidable task. My team, unknown to anyone in the world, received the well-deserved eminence and recognition, and we became celebrities in the universe of space exploration. My team, and myself as the team leader, were all over the news. But it occurred to me that Audi could have easily taken that stardom and prominence for herself if she'd chosen to announce our triumph. Instead, she asked me to do it.

"When I failed, the leadership took the responsibility for my failure, but when I succeeded, the leadership gave me the entire credit. I learned a big lesson from that episode which no school or university will ever teach. No level of education will ever teach such a meritorious gesture, and it is every employee's dream to work in such a company, under such great leadership.

"For the first year-and-half or so, our fledgling space program had nothing but failures and Audi was the face of all SYMBIOSIS's embarrassments. But after our first success, Audi was never seen on media, and individual employees and teams became the face of our company. Every occasion where Audi could have gained popularity, recognition, and stature, she instead gave it to her employees. In return, she gained the trust and love of us all. More importantly, over all these years, I have known her to be genuinely happy for the successes and achievements of others, and not even once felt that others are taking away her fame."

I was enraptured by that story, still vividly picturing the press conference Ethan gave after their first major coup. I was watching it with my parents. Before that day in February 2021, I wasn't paying any attention to any science news. So I never saw Audi on any of the SYMBIOSIS press releases. I'd always assumed that since Audi was shy, she was sending in her team to handle the media and the news. Now I knew the full story.

After hearing what Ethan said, my heart craved to see Audi. I knew I would see her the following day at our high school reunion, but I just couldn't control myself. Although our reunion is organized once every five years and in a different city each time, I was attending for the first time. The reunion was usually in July, but this one had been postponed until December.

I told Ethan how badly I wanted to see Audi, emphasizing that I could not wait until the reunion the next day to see her. Ethan checked his watch and said, "Well, we have a town hall meeting in about ten minutes to commemorate the ten-year anniversary of the establishment of SYMBIOSIS. Audi is addressing the employees and new graduates. I can arrange a seat for you."

At around 2:30PM, I was sitting in the auditorium waiting for the town hall meeting to start. Employees were gradually filling the seats. I could see in their faces that they were eager to hear Audi speak. I pulled out my phone as I waited, deciding to start attempting to decode the quote from Abi's office door. It seemed emblematic of all Abi was made of. Clearly, I thought, the DNA double helix structure embedded with musical notes implies that music is in her DNA. The chemical bonds indicate that her expertise is in biology and life sciences.

The enigmatic symbolization reminded me how eccentric Audi was. Though Audi was now famous and wealthy, she was just an ordinary girl back in high school, very simply dressed and with nothing to her appearance that arrest any attention. In fact, she was so nondescript that many, including myself, passed by her in the school corridor without any consideration or a second look. But what had initially captivated me towards Audi was when she talked.

I recalled the first time I paid attention to Audi, in tenth grade English Literature. We were asked to write an essay profiling the life and achievements of a famous person as part of a language arts practice. With the exception of a girl named Clarisse, who wrote a beautiful speech but ultimately couldn't face the stage and fainted, everyone else in class spoke about celebrities, Nobel laureates, pop stars, or princesses. But Audi's pick was unconventional.

While nearly the entire class practiced unswerving circumlocution to reach the minimum word count set by our teacher and made sleep-inducing, soporific speeches, Audi's essay was conversely straightforward and captivating. There wasn't a slightest hesitation in her pellucid speech, as she perfectly enunciated her superbly written and thoroughly researched speech. The introduction was indelibly etched in my memory. Without daunting and with immense gratitude to the value of the words, she started by saying, "Today, I am going to talk about a person whom you probably have never heard of before. He was not perfect, but he was unique. His philosophy and principles belonged to a new breed. He was not a celebrity, a rock star, nor a politician. Though he was nominated for the Nobel Prize five different times, he was not awarded one. He stood for truth and forged an invincible weapon called "Satyagraha." With his theory that violence can only beget and foment more violence and can never bring an end to it, he developed his philosophy of nonviolence and pioneering principles of passive resistance, and waged a peaceful war that led to the independence of his country.

"By bringing independence to his country without bloodshed, he showcased with unimpeachable evidence the power of his impregnable weapon of nonviolence, inspired peaceful movements for freedom and civil rights, and a humane way to combat and eradicate the deeply rooted disease of racism and prejudice across the world. He was imprisoned and awarded several jail sentences, but paradoxically, his confinement and incarceration became a badge of honor for him and his followers. With his belief that even the most hardened hearts and minds are capable of change through gestures of love, he changed the entire world and became the symbol of peace and freedom in the 20th century.

"Albert Einstein once said, and I quote, 'Generations to come will scarce believe that such a one as this ever in flesh and blood walked upon this Earth'. As humanity wept when he died, he showed us that humility and truth are more powerful than empires. Dignitaries from all over the world attended his funeral in veneration and love. He never held a political position, nor amassed wealth or property, but he died as the richest man of character the world has seen in the last twenty centuries. In an ardent attempt to educate the future generations the inescapable fate of a tough oppressor when confronted by an apostle of nonviolence, and to unlock the secrets behind the limitless power of a frail man who renounced wealth and rank, countless biographers wrote books about him. As a man of all races and religions, his memorials were built all over the world."

AUDRIANNA

udi went on with the essay without disclosing the name of the famous person until the end, which kept all the students and even the teacher intrigued and engaged to what she was saying. Despite Audi's uncommon yet gripping format, our dour teacher gave her a "B" because her speech didn't meet the requirements outlined and the format accentuated. The format of the speech was to introduce the person and then speak about them. The teacher gave Audi the option to redo the paper for a higher grade, but Audi never very much cared about petty grades. For her, education and knowledge were always more important than superficial scores.

When we were about to graduate from high school, I remember asking Audi in my classic condescending tone - "Were you always this eccentric?"

Instead of getting offended for calling her idiosyncratic, Audi simply laughed and said, "No, no...when I was little, I was just like any other ordinary girl. My favorite color was changing every day, favorite book was changing every week, favorite TV show was changing every month, and my life ambitions were changing every six months from a waitress to becoming a doctor, and from a zoo keeper to an FBI agent. I used to ride my bike after I went home from school, play with my friends, and when it was time to do homework, I used to malinger and come up with silly excuses of headache, stomach ache, or would randomly pick from the wide palette of body pains. As a typical insolent girl, when things didn't go my way, or something was hard, or when I was told to do something that I didn't want to do, I used to get restive, and being peevish and petulant, I would vent out my anger and frustration by stomping my feet and slamming the doors.

"We are a big family and I am the middle child out of five. We are considerably far from being considered as a rich family, but we never had issues with finding money for food. We didn't take expensive vacations and we spent all our summers at our grandparents' quaint home. As years passed by with my carefree attitude, on the evening of Friday, the 15th April of 2011, exactly a week from my fifteenth birthday, my dad walked into my room with a package. There was a gift wrap around it, so I couldn't see what was inside. But the way he was carrying it, I had a pretty good idea of what was in it. I was super excited and impatient to open it as my dad promised to give me a laptop for my birthday.

"My dad definitely got my complete attention by displaying the gift. I was quietly expecting him to hand me the gift as he promised and walk away, instead, he sat down in a chair and asked me, 'What do you want to do when you grow up?'

"I was quietly stunned as I had not anticipated any questions. I sensed he was trying to mock me, so I said something like, 'I want to earn a lot money. I want to be the richest person on Earth. No, no wait, I want to be the richest person in the solar system.'

"My dad simply smiled, relaxed a bit in the chair, and asked, 'Can you name the richest person in 1937?' I was initially rattled by the question, but ultimately, I was honest and carelessly blurted out: 'I don't know.' My eyes were only on the gift and all I wanted was to open it. Then he asked me if maybe I knew the richest person from that decade. I kept wondering when would this small talk be over. After a while I murmured, 'I don't know', and I started to feel embarrassed as I couldn't answer both his questions.

"He then took a deep breath, expanded the question, and asked, 'How about any affluent person in the first half of the 20th century?'

"I decided to think about the answer for a while. As he kept staring into my eyes, time started to hang heavily on me. Despite the longevity of my deep and immersive thinking to recall a name, my reply was still the same as before. I shamefully mumbled as I admitted I didn't know. I couldn't look into his eyes anymore.

"As I lowered my head feeling ashamed and staring at the floor looking diminished, he then asked me to name three famous people from the first half of the 20th century. Without thinking, I raised my face, met his gaze, and ticked off the first three people that popped into my head: Albert Einstein, Nikola Tesla and Marie Curie.

"My father simply said, 'There you go!' and handed me the gift. He then took his wallet out, pulled out a $100 bill, kept it on the top of the gift and said, 'If you still want to become the richest person, here is your initial capital investment.' He then kissed my forehead, and with a pride on his face that I would make the right decision, left my room.

"The whole conversation lasted only about five minutes. The excitement I had five minutes before, when I got the first glimpse at the gift, was all dead. I didn't comprehend what my dad meant. I didn't understand what his point was right then. But I couldn't get it out of my mind and it kept me deliberating. I contemplated the said exercise for the next few days, not even bothering to open my gift or taking the money that was sitting on the top of it. It sat in my room, where I gazed at it for several days.

"When I finally construed what my dad was trying to teach me, it instantly transformed me into a complete new person. It propelled me into studying every book I could find in my home, in school, and in the public library. I never spent the $100 he gave me. It is still with me to this day."

* * *

Although Audi caught my attention early in the tenth grade, I hadn't cared much about her then as I was outrageously self-absorbed; and in fact, I bullied her- and others- during the majority of high school. However, I could relate her early transformation to her becoming a trailblazer in space exploration, but only much later in my life. During high school, Audi became an avid reader. She was reading all sorts of books and most of them were on science and technology. She really got into and devoured science fiction stories. I remember her saying that she wanted to start the next age of exploration. It was an impossible task, but she believed that her goal was within reach. Things that most people generally believe impossible, Audi believes genuinely possible and also convinced to the point of being a fanatic. Though she didn't have the abilities, talents, and technical prowess to do it back then in high school, she had the self-confidence and belief in herself. Audi wasn't a particularly gifted or a precocious child. She was just like any other girl. Obviously, she must have developed her iconoclastic attitude over time by challenging herself with a 'possible' mindset.

Audi was always laconic and kept her words few, but there is sincerity in all she says. I initially thought her hesitancy in conversation was because she was diffident. But much later I learned that her habit of economy and frugality of words is because she doesn't want a careless or an inconsiderate thought escaping her tongue. And it is no surprise that a person who is thrifty and stingy with their words will be thorough and meticulous in their speech, weighing every word.

While I was lost in my thoughts, the whole crowd exploded into a deafening applause. Audi had entered the auditorium, and everyone stood in deference as she walked towards the rostrum to begin her speech. I was delighted to see her after such a long time and she looked exactly as I remembered from our college days: very simple. The whole auditorium fell into utter silence as she approached the lectern to commence her formal address.

"Welcome everyone. Today, we celebrate the ten-year anniversary of **SYMBIOSIS** Corporation. Though **SYMBIOSIS** means 'mutually beneficial relationship', we are more than that. Our company stands for synergy. As you all know, **SYMBIOSIS** is a different kind of company. We have always repudiated the norms. We have always questioned the status quo. We have always grilled the existing theories. We have always pioneered new approaches. We have always challenged ourselves. We always strive for culture of excellence and innovation. We, **SYMBIOSIS**, has begun the fourth age of exploration. With slow and incremental progress, it took us time to get here, and to accomplish impressive feats. In the process, we had our share of many failures and some successes. But the remarkable thing is, we continued to learn from our mistakes without giving up.

"Today, we also have here the fresh graduates from the class of 2029, whom our company has supported for their education. They all graduated as the cream of their class and are now looking for employment opportunities. Some of them have already received job offers, while others are still looking. I wish them all the very best in their future endeavors.

"Education is the basic building block and the foundation upon which we can build a better future and solve the difficult problems we face. My father and I always believed that education transcends us through every barrier, and schools are the conduits for knowledge. As such, our company is proud to associate with institutions around the world in supporting students achieving their educational goals. We also believe that each child is unique, and with right principles they are all leaders in their own way. I am sure by now you all have read a lot of inspirational books which taught you how to live with passion and purpose. But as your graduation gift, I am going to impart some lessons I learned from my personal life experiences, and I hope they help you lead a better life. I will also succinctly share my vision for the necessity of space exploration.

"When I was growing up, a lot of people told me that I was atypical, and some even called me eccentric. But it did not deter me from my goal. It takes courage to think differently and do something new. It takes courage to travel an unexplored path and work on something deemed impossible. While the world around you is trying its best to make you like everyone else, you must overcome that internal struggle to conform, and allow your vision to drive you for the rest of your life.

"Almost eighteen years ago, when I was in ninth grade, my father taught me a lesson. It was a simple lesson, but it profoundly influenced me. He taught me that wealth follows knowledge, not the other way around. But he gave me a $100 bill in case it was still wealth I was seeking. I still have that $100 bill to this day. I learned then that no one remembers the richest person in the world. But for some obscure reason, people still equate success with money. It is bizarre, but it is quite natural for the human brain to be obsessed with amassing more and more wealth, beyond one's needs and wants. Hoarding money became a mad rush, a distinguishing characteristic, and a matter of prestige in our modern civilization. Of all the human inventions, it turns out that money is the most alluring, addictive and untiring game ever invented. Added to that, our mind is a restless beast. The more we indulge in possessing money, the more the mind wants, fermenting us into a vicious cycle of dissatisfaction and restlessness. Money has that enslaving quality, and I am not immune to it either. And when my mind goes towards becoming affluent, I look at the $100 bill that my dad gave me. It is a constant reminder for me why I wanted to do what I do. My lesson to you today is: *why* you want to accomplish is far more important than *what* you want to accomplish.

"By the time I graduated with an accelerated master's degree in May 2019, I had worked hard to acquire the required knowledge, and also set my future goals. I even had a clear vision on how to design, develop and launch my innovative ideas into a successful and viable business. I was aspiring high. My friend Abigail and I saved a good amount of money by creating and selling an app, but it wasn't enough. I needed an investor, but I had trouble finding one. My ideas were too futuristic for many investors at that time when the space industry was still nascent. Every potential investor rejected me, but I remained bold and undeterred.

"It was one of the hardest battles in my life, but I kept going door to door, from early in the morning to sunset, knocking every entrance I could find to convince every investor I could approach that my ideas were viable. It helps to have someone else believe in you, trust in you, in achieving your goals regardless of how bad it gets. It pushes you towards attaining your goal when you feel tired or feel like giving up. I do have one such person in my life, and it is my graduate professor, who is now one of the board of directors.

"I was out of college at that time, and I didn't want to be a burden to anyone. During the day time I was seeking for investors, and in the evenings, I was waiting tables at a nearby restaurant and then later sleeping in Abigail's room. It was an exhausting struggle with ruthless and disheartening rejections for about six months, but ultimately my perseverance paid off. It was then I learned that to evolve into a leader, one should not only lead into uncharted territory without flinching or becoming daunted by temporary disappointments and failures, but one also should persist and persevere in the face of what appears to be like insurmountable obstacles. Being a leader is not an easy thing. Leaders should be able to endure a lot of pain in the face of impediments and still be driven to fight back in times of distress. A leader must be an explorer maintaining focus despite a deluge of worries. My lesson to you here is: more than the success, a leader should know how to handle failures – whether professionally or in personal life. Finally, I established this company in December 2019, and today we are celebrating ten years of learning from our failures. And my advice for the first step in becoming a good leader with exceptional leadership skills is taking the responsibility for failures, and giving the success, fame, and victory to the team."

I searched the crowd for Ethan's face, but could not see him. Audi paused here, seeming to accent what she'd just said without any idea that Ethan and I had discussed this very concept less than an hour before.

"What makes you unique and attractive to potential employers," Audi continued, "is your outside-the-box thinking. Once you enter a company, it doesn't matter where you got your degree from, or what your academic credentials are. All that matters is, 'can you make and deliver the product?' That is the difference between theory and practice. A good example of out-of-box thinking is RD-180. For decades, oxygen rich staged combustion cycle engines were considered practically impossible due to the high-pressure oxygen rich propellant being a powerful oxidizer which corrodes the metal quickly. But with some out of the box thinking, ingenious and clever metallurgy with titanium alloys, we got the extremely efficient, low weight, high performance RD-180 rocket engine. Remember, revolutionary thinking begins with someone believing that a problem is impossible to solve. And always keep in mind that all breakthrough scientific revelations were the result of paradigm-shifting, transformative ideas that warped and ruptured the accepted thinking in trying to solve the anomalies.

"Do you remember the history lesson of manufacturing economics where in 1940s and 1950s American manufacturing mindset was either we can have a high-quality product or a low-cost product, but not both? But at the same time, Japan, rising from the ashes of World War II, had shown that both reliability and affordability are possible. It's that thinking that revolutionized the manufacturing industry. Things we take for granted today like UV water purifiers, plastic roads, and passive vaccine storage devices were all the results of someone's consideration of creative ideas for costly problems, and their vision and willingness to alter the existing reality by inventing better solutions that never existed with ideas that ran against conventional wisdom. So, my lesson here is that your thinking and response to problems determines who you really are.

"As for my views on the necessity of space exploration, I am sure by now you all are tired of the platitude that space exploration stimulates curiosity and inspires youth to study science and engineering to develop cutting-edge technologies which then eventually will drive the economy. Though it is true, there is a bigger reason and it has to do with the bleaker future for the human species. The grand history of Earth has episodes that rattled and menaced life, and for all we know so far, we are alone in this universe. Besides us, there is no evidence of life elsewhere. The universe appears to be lonely and dead. Life on Earth started from dead chemistry, assembled into self-replicating patterns, and became very complex over eons of time. We, humans, are the result of that millions of years of evolution. We are complex beings with unique features of intelligence and undisciplined imagination. Our Earth was once home to a host of human species that coexisted with one another. Whatever the reason, all other humankind's antecedents became extinct, and for the first time in millions of years of human evolutionary history, we are the only human species still extant. Among other reasons, a pandemic disease can completely efface us out, the only surviving human species from the face of Earth and given what we know so far, perhaps there would be no intelligent life left in the universe. If it scares you, you understand the gravity of the situation. So, we should undertake exploration and permanent settlements on other planets for the most basic reason: our self-preservation. Humanity's survival and continuity is simply too precious for us to fall back into complacency and do nothing.

"I believe that we are at a juncture that space exploration, which was once a domain of science fiction and a scientific possibility, has now become a necessity and inevitable for long-term survival and the future of our human race. Before concerns escalate and exacerbate, we need to radically rethink about humanity's future without being trapped on this tiny mud ball in an eternal universe. In addition, there are questions that still baffle and bewilder us to this day such as how life emerged on Earth and why Earth was conducive for the origin, survival and persistence of life. In the process of our exploration, we may also find life beyond Earth and an answer to a fundamental question: Is life ubiquitous throughout the universe?

"So, as I wrap up, I would like you not to forget a few things. As we close our operations for the year to relish some family time and to recharge and energize ourselves, let us not forget that though we are mavericks, we symbolize *synergy*. Let us not forget the 'why' behind our efforts. Let us not forget that we grow stronger by embracing each other's wonders and weaknesses. And finally, let us not forget that though everyone has talent, your reasoning and response to a problem dictates who you really are - as therein lies all our growth.

"I hope you and your family have joyful winter holidays, and I wish you all the very best in your endeavors."

Pellucid in style as always and a riveting oration, I burst into applause along with the rest of the audience, who collectively endorsed her address with plaudits and fervid acclamation. I was probably the first one to start applauding, Audi looked over and noticed me sitting in Ethan's reserved seat, and I could sense that she was elated to see me. She walked down from the podium, came straight to me, and enveloped me in a big hug. The applause still resounding, Audi whispered to me, "Abigail told me that you are here for an interview. Let's all catch up this evening at my house. I'll send a car to your hotel around 6."

Audi squeezed my hand before moving on to others in the audience, connecting with and engaging with people individually.

An impeccable speaker and with her empowering speech, she seamlessly implanted the seed of *why* we are doing of what we are doing. As I watched her, I wondered why Audi talked about her post-college existence, which was probably the lowest point in her life. She could have spoken of the success stories and the good times when the company made gazillion dollars in profit. But she chose to talk about her struggles and rejections. I guessed it was to teach others that before achieving success, one needs to taste failure. Of course, failure is a bitter pill to everyone. However, in the pursuit of anything meaningful, irrespective of the outcome, the journey itself is an exacting teacher testing and giving valuable lessons. More than that I guess, it was also to teach how one picks up from failures and moves forward determines what they really are made of.

During Audi's speech, the unconscious part of my brain was decrypting Abi's quote in the background. I realized now that the quote appeared to be in the form of a pyramid. The mystery surrounding how and why the Egyptian pyramids were constructed is still not solved, but we didn't quit, and we kept on curiously probing for answers. So, I speculated that the cryptic message written using Greek letters and musical notes must be about her restless curiosity and her never quitting attitude.

Unquestionably, the human brain represents 'think', but why did Abi use an electrical circuit inside the brain? As I started to look closely at the circuit with voltage and current connected to a bulb, my thinking bulb glowed inside my brain that the message in fact is Watt, which is voltage x current, but being used for similar sounding word 'what'. As I moved to the rhombus shape on the last line, I knew those shapes are widely used in flowcharts and the rhombus or the diamond shape stands for 'if'. Just before I thought I deduced, I realized that it was not 'if', but actually is 'then' as I noticed the flowchart symbol connected down to 'do not disturb' symbol.

Though I worked out the conundrum, I need to ascertain and validate my conclusions. On my way out, I quickly walked towards Abi's office and turned the frame around, finding exactly what I expected to read: "***If you think what I am doing is impossible, then don't disturb me.***" Over the years, I have read several positive quotations in my life, but Abi's quote is definitely the pinnacle of my list of favorite quotes. And it is unquestionably true that the dichotomy between people who achieve and those who do not achieve things is the difference in their mindsets, attitudes, and the personal beliefs and theories they develop about themselves, and of what is possible, and what is not.

If you think what
I am doing is
impossible, then don't
disturb me

RADHA

With a gratifying feeling about my time at **SYMBIOSIS** and a general confidence about my interview performance, I was back in my hotel room by 4PM. I called my parents and, at their urging, narrated every detail of the interview. Laila was back from school, and Luke had just woken up from his nap, they melted me with their winsome smiles.

Overcome by lassitude and feeling somnolent from fatigue, I decided to take a short power nap but ended up sleeping for about an hour. With a groggy head, I took a bath cycling through warm and cold water to invigorate myself. It was only about a thirty-minute ride from my hotel to Audi's home and as I watched the Phoenix suburbs whizz by, I found myself thinking about my history with the old friends I was headed to meet.

Though I feel proud to have attended Harvard in general, a significant part of the reason for my pride was Abi and Audi. My parents never called me names or labeled me "lazy" or "stupid", but they would sometimes compare my grades to Abi's or my diligence to Audi's—to my detriment, of course. This comparison diminished my confidence, and I slowly came to think of myself as inferior to Abi and Audi. As a result, I stopped trying to show my parents what I was capable of. We are usually amazed when we see in others the traits we lack in ourselves, but we also, and especially during the teenage years, grow envy of them. Correspondingly, I developed animosity towards Abi and Audi, and grew jealous of them. Though we didn't have a great relationship to start with, it grew more acrimonious when I started bullying them. I never went to extremes, but I'm positive I hurt their feelings.

Similarly, I developed hatred towards my parents. I was a typical teenage girl, deftly surfing the hormonal tides and quietly sailing through all the modern endemic teenage challenges, both real and hypothetical. Jerked around by innocuous hormones and at the mercy of my mercurial mood, sometimes I felt apathetic and nonchalant, and other times caring and concerned; sometimes I felt befuddled and stuck in a morass, and other times clear and composed. But the biggest anomaly was that I felt both confident and scared at the same time. And like a typical teenager, I felt my parents' were anachronistic, belonging to the age of dinosaurs, and are out of touch with contemporary life.

As I enthusiastically enrolled into the turbulent years of teens during which time ennui was not in my dictionary as so much drama was happening, I felt like an adult who was able to fend for myself and make my own decisions. As a matter of fact, I never cared to listen to advice or suggestions from my parents and other adults, and I was notorious for giving circuitous answers and curt replies to the most well-intentioned guidance.

As a youth, I'd been branded dependent on my parents, and hence, in my struggle for independence, identity and popularity, I became rebellious, ignoring and avoiding my mom and dad. At every turn, I rejected their ideas in partisan favor of my own.

Whenever I was reminded about studying better and working harder, I accused them of being nosy and encroaching on my private space. Even so, living in an envelop of a fantasy world, I isolated myself from the struggles my parents had to go through to buy me whatever I wanted even when the cost was prohibitive. Though they were always amenable to my desires and never said "no" to anything I asked them, I never bothered to ask myself how two lower-middle class parents were able to buy all that expensive stuff. I got everything I wanted, from clothes to electronics. At the dinner table, where I was always on my phone even when they tried to make a conversation, all I had to do was show them the latest dress I wanted on the screen, mid-call. In the next couple of days, the new dress would be in my closet.

Daughters are known to be notorious for making their fathers play to their tunes, and I was no exception. Whenever I saw the latest phone on the market, I had my dad pre-order it for me, even knowing he did dishes by hand in order to save power by not operating the dishwasher. I never knew how much the mortgage or the phone bill cost, and my parents seemed to never worry about themselves or their own future, instead saving everything they could for my college education. I was their first and only priority, and they complied with my every mandate. They never forced me to help with the daily chores. Instead of gratitude though, I only became more stubborn and rude.

I never cared about the work that my mom put into stitching new clothes for me. I was so self-obsessed that I couldn't even appreciate her niftiness. She spent entire nights after a long work day and most of her weekends making me clothes. I never even considered why I got new clothes whenever I wanted, and was always just eager to flaunt my new threads and self-aggrandize my status for whom I considered my adoring public. As I shined in new clothes, I abased Audi for wearing the same old out-of-style attire.

I didn't realize that my mom and dad came home from work to attend to my every whimsy, prepare dinner, and prep for the next day, whereas I had only one job: to study. Instead of giving them the respite they deserved from their already hectic lives, I created additional work. My hedonistic ways mired me so deeply in superficial pleasures that my education became secondary, and at one point I developed a deep aversion to any form of study. I was exclusively interested in my appearance to stay contemporary with ever changing dynamical fashion, and to retain my popularity so as to control the girl groups.

Late in tenth grade, while suffering from low attendance and failing grades, my parents were notified to meet the principal. That meeting changed everything. Adding to the reproves by the principal, my parents gave me an ultimatum: they would not fund my college studies unless I started to take school more seriously and improve my grades. At that point, I should have said the gig was up and gotten serious. Instead, my reaction was that of a typical teenager expressing disdain - I got angry, stormed to my room, and slammed the door. That was the day I started hating my parents. In addition to an abrupt aberration in the treatment and acute reproach to which I was unaccustomed, they also rescinded many privileges, imposing sanctions that felt foreign. Eventually, my phone was taken and I was not allowed to go out with friends or even visit their homes.

Revoking my freedom fanned the fire of hatred burning in me. I came to the conclusion that they never loved me and were forcibly imposing their interests on to me, instead of embracing who I wanted to be. I pejoratively criticized them endlessly, and only wanted to leave home and go as far as possible, never to see them again.

Knowing my plight, Ethan staged an intervention, and despite my deplorable bullying and general nastiness towards Abi and Audi, they gave me a pep talk. Appealing to my basest ideals, they reminded me that studying would help me get away from my parents and set me up for my future, providing the opportunity to kill two birds with one stone. I made it my mission to get into a college far from Chicago, and with a steadfast ambition of keeping my grades up and achieving a good SAT score, I decided to follow Abi and Audi's footsteps and buried my head in books for the rest of high school. Ultimately, that resulted in admission to Harvard University, along with Audi and Ethan. Abi opted to attend nearby MIT. Their help in getting me into Harvard cured me of the jealousy I had of them and I was even able to convince Audi to be my roommate in the dorms.

Ethan's major was Space Technology with a minor in Art, which I considered a bizarre combination. Abigail opted to major in Life Sciences with minor in Music. Contemplating my options, I opted to major in Journalism. And because of my interest in etymology, I decided to minor in English Literature.

We had no idea what Audi's major was. She was a maverick with an unquenchable thirst for knowledge and an insatiable appetite for learning, so it could have been anything. She studied everything and took seemingly every class in the university's catalog from Science to Mechanics, Literature to Engineering, and Archaeology to Astronomy. Her philosophy was simple: there is no such thing as useless education. For her, education was not about filling the brain with stuff, but instead about igniting a thirst for reasoning and the thought process was everything. She incessantly exercised her mind as though she was in perennial apprehension that she would lose it if she didn't. Learning never ended for her. Her credo was that there was always something to learn and there is no limit to the knowledge one can acquire. To that end, she worked in the library all four years of college, voraciously reading every book she could. Likewise, Abi's exceptional resume and full scholarship got her a plum post as a research assistant and worked all four years of college in a world-class Biology research lab.

Ethan was not as lucky. During the first and second years of college, unable to get other positions, he endured hardship mopping hallways and cleaning restrooms in the undergraduate dining halls and working as a barista in a coffee shop. I felt pity that Ethan was relegated to hard labor, but by third year, with his excellent GPA, he'd sufficiently impressed everyone in his department to receive a teaching assistant position. In addition, being didactic by nature, I was unsurprised that he also worked part-time as an online tutor, which paid him well. Besides being industrious, I also knew Ethan to be extremely inquisitive, a hands-on experimental type of a person. He had always been the type of person who would pull apart the pieces of a pedestal trash can to understand firsthand how pushing down the pedal causes the lid to open, and how the soft-close system actually works. Or the type of person who, as the flight attendant demonstrates how to operate the life vest in case of an emergency, would actually request to actively participate. He prefers to perform new tasks once with his own hands than observe someone else perform it a million times. He was also a techie who could easily pull apart and piece together a watch or a camera. Accordingly, he became a hardware expert, and because of his perspicacity and sound insight, he was the go-to person in our circle of friends for any issues with electronics.

I ranked Audi and Abi as equivalent in their cerebral capacity. They were intellectual peers and practical visionaries, and there was always a vigorous but friendly competition between the two erudites. Though they rivaled each other intellectually, Abi was always at the top of the class, while Audi cared little about superficial grades. Audi was a polymath, specifically adroit at solving problems using approaches from multiple disciplines and coming up with eclectic solutions. Abi, on the other hand, was a multifaceted and well-rounded person, into everything from academics to art to chess—adept at anything but sports. Audi was a person of few words, but when she spoke, she had already pondered the problem, examined it a thousand different ways, and puts herself in the best position to offer a cogent decision. Abi on the other hand, was chatty and loquacious, and would talk her way through issues running her thought turbine, offering a myriad ways to problem-solve in the meantime.

Nevertheless, Audi and Abi were different; but far from the complete antithesis to one another. Both were assiduous and peers in perseverance and compassion. After our second-year summer break in 2016, Abi returned disturbed from visiting her family in Chicago. Audi and Ethan were also back from a summer internship, revitalized and ready to kick start the new academic year. During summer break, Abi learned from her younger sister, Yeva Roy, an athlete attending another Ivy League school, that some of her athlete friends suffered sexual abuse perpetrated by some powerful people they trusted in the confines of the four walls. The student-athletes were worried about potential retaliation and repercussions of accusing without any proof, the damage that would emanate, and the detrimental effects to their scholarships and careers.

When Abi shared this, my initial thought was to ask if anyone had recorded anything untoward. By 2016, everyone carried a phone and recording misdeeds was becoming increasingly prevalent. But the longer I thought, the more apparent the problem appeared. Who carries a phone during intense sports practice? It was most likely that when the athlete was assaulted, their phone was in a locker or some other place away from the training area. Even within the confines of a small room, a student may not be able to reach their phone.

We were all unsettled by Abi's report, but Audi saw an opportunity, a need to fill. An athlete may not have a phone on hand, but they all wore activity trackers nearly all the time, save perhaps while taking a shower. Audi got to work with the intention of writing a code that would add functionality to fitness trackers to activate a distress call in the wearer's phone. However, Audi soon sampled failure when she learned that GPS fitness trackers and watches at that time could only connect to phones from a short distance to each other. They also did not have the ability to directly place phone calls. Audi saw a bigger opportunity to combine GPS and cellular capability into one device. She recruited Ethan into the project. Being a hardware expert, he bought off-the-shelf parts from the money he earned from his internship and built a wearable device, for which Audi wrote software code.

In addition to GPS and phone capability, the device included a continuous heart rate and blood pressure monitor, microphone and micro-speakers, and other functionalities that an athlete would need to track their progress all day. And when an abuse is perceived, the user would manually press an inconspicuous button on the device which would call the local police, automatically activate the microphone so they can listen in to the act and send them the GPS location.

But because Ethan used readily available parts, the device was bulky, and nowhere close to the slim fitness trackers and watches available on the market. It took them almost a year for a working prototype. When Ethan showed it to me, I laughed as it looked like a house arrest ankle monitor. Audi and Ethan even tried to sell it, spending all the money they earned from their internship, but there was no buyer and they quickly went bust.

Despite the utter failure, Audi was not dispirited. Her somberness from forlorn attempts was outweighed by her penchant for resolving the problem and providing a solution. As cellular capable smart watches started to trickle into the market, Audi decided to use the code she wrote for her failed product and create an app. With help from Abi, she created a tractable app that she called "AA". In the event of an abuse, but only when explicitly selected by the user, the app records the audio conversation and physiological trauma responses in the body such as heart rate and blood pressure and stores them as evidence. Audi and Abi made some money selling the app, a copious amount for a college student. Using Abi's research data, they even added a functionality where the app would activate on its own when a specific combination of physiological responses was detected by the smart watch. As the app became a hit, they added voice recognition with user-set distress code so that the app could be activated when the user could not manually activate it. The versatility of the app is, it is so adaptable that it could be installed on any activity tracker.

While my friends kept themselves busy, I did not work during college as I knew my parents had opened a college fund for me when I was a child. I decided to live on that. Though the money my parents saved was more than enough for my college expenses, it quickly evaporated and was barely sufficient to support my opulent lifestyle. Lucky for me, my boyfriend Philip was affluent and had no shortage of money.

While I was absent in my thoughts and paying no attention to where I was going, the car suddenly announced that I was reaching the destination shortly. "You will reach your destination in 90 seconds," a voice declared, and it took me a moment to recognize the British-accented voice's origin. The red letters of the car's time management display had begun flashing, counting down. "Eighty-one, eighty, seventy-nine...". I became anxious to see how the home of the CEO of a behemoth corporation would look. I was even more curious since I knew Audi's tastes and preferences. Soon the car stopped in front of a house and the doors unlocked automatically. It was an ordinary single-family house. The house was markedly smaller in size than I fantasized. I imagined in my mind that the house of a CEO with plenitude of wealth would be a luxurious mansion, but the house before me was conspicuously simple looking. I wondered if it was the correct house or not.

The roof was made of solar tiles and a sparkling LED lightshow was dancing on the facade as an ornamentation and an invitation for the winter holidays. As I trod dubiously towards the front door, I noticed assorted plants, shrubs and trees arranged in a grand scheme on either side of the pathway. Skeptical if it was Audi's home or not, I hesitantly pressed the doorbell and peeked inside through the lucid glass panels on the side of the front door. As I took a glimpse inside, my mind settled. From what I could see, every corner echoed Audi. Within about ten seconds, with a big warm hug, I received an effusive welcome from Audi into her beautiful home. While walking me to her living room, Audi asked me how I was doing and how the interview went. I said that I was doing great and was very confident that a favorable outcome would come from my interview. Audi was glad to hear my confidence.

I was thinking the house interior would be extravagant and flamboyant, but it wasn't lavish as I thought. We walked through her home office before going to the living room. Audi's office was impeccable. Not a single piece of paper was out of place. Pencils and pens were arranged in groups and pointing the same direction. With a video conferencing setup on one side of the room, the other side was organized perfectly by stacks of books. The wall-to-ceiling bookshelf was replete with books ranging from astrophysics to anthropology and autobiographies to fantasy novels; some in pristine condition and some battered. I was pretty sure it is only one of the many bookshelves in the house. The walls were painted in bold and refreshing colors but were not garish at all. Patently, there was no color coordination and looked more like a natural fusion. An interior decorator would have fainted from the bizarre blend, but I loved it. Right next to the bookshelf was a display of distinct terrariums of diverse sizes suffused with air plants. Nothing in the office was just to embellish the room; the items were both decorative and utilitarian.

Adjacent to her office was a room with limpid glass doors and what appeared to be a lush and verdant vertical hydroponic farm. As I walked towards the living room, I noticed that every corner was filled with plants, and every wall was adorned with array of picture frames of Audi and her siblings with their parents. There was no sign if she was married and has kids. Though I shared a room with her during college, I'd always found Audi was extremely reticent and kept her personal life to herself. But the impression I got was that for Audi, marriage and kids were a distraction, and she would rather spend time inventing and creating opportunities.

Though I have broad latitude with her, I dared not to ask if she is yet married or not. But almost as though she read my mind, Audi told me that she lives with her younger siblings who were out that day for a graduation party.

It was hard not to notice the advanced technology in every facet of the house, which only seemed magical to me. It appeared as if Audi had created a mini research center and her house was a testing ground of their technologies where she continually tests and improves. In short, the house was a commingling of nature and technology, and the disposition of items can be summed up in two words- "organized chaos."

I walked into the living room to see a structure which looked like the model for Mars habitation module that I saw in **SYMBIOSIS** website. The room was simple yet polished, small yet capacious, with sparse stuff yet efficient with all the amenities at one's fingertips. There was already someone waiting there and to my surprise it was Radha. We went to high school together. While Ethan, Audi, Abi and I went to Boston for college, Radha stayed back in Chicago. After I left Chicago post-high school, I lost touch with her.

Squealing with delight, I ran towards Radha and hugged her in astonishment. Radha told me that she is now a chef, specializing in vegan dishes. She was there for the reunion but had stopped by Audi's home to make Audi some new vegan dishes that she had created.

Just then Audi got a phone call and excused herself and left the room. Out of earnest curiosity, I asked Radha what made her become a chef. "I got inspiration to become a vegan chef on two separate occasions in my life," she said. "The first time was in high school. My mother is a foodie and wanted to become a chef. But my grandparents, who were dogmatic, did not encourage her, and like so many other women of her generation, she buried her dreams. But after her marriage, my father exhorted and bolstered my mom to attend culinary training programs and classes.

"She loved to make a variety of savory dishes for us. We were not vegetarian. We used to eat all sorts of animal meats and seafoods. And if the TV in our home was on, it was on one of the food channels. Because we all got to eat yummy delicious food, no one in our home dared to change the channel. We all used to watch what my mom watched, which was any of the multiple food channels featuring international recipes, cooking techniques, and tips.

"One day, we were watching a competition show on one of the food channels where the chefs must prepare a meal for a large group of people attending a convention. The challenge was to use only vegetarian items, no meat and no seafood. One of the two chef's in the competition was considered an Avenger in the chefs' world. He was a highly reputable chef and never lost a competition. My mom practically adored him. She never missed a show of his.

"When it was revealed that the chefs must prepare dishes with only vegetables and no meat should be used, his facial expression started to change. He looked at the vegetables and went berserk, but just shy of destructively violent. Unable to cook vegetarian food, he went foul-mouthed and said he never cooked vegetarian food and it is disgusting. My mother was in a complete shock when she heard the chef's flippant remarks. She felt that there were several reasons why people chose to be vegetarian: some for health reasons, others for cultural, tradition, ethical, religious, or spiritual reasons. She also asserted that the chef's devalue of vegetarian food reflected not only of him, but also of his parents and what his teachers taught him.

"My mom sent an email to the TV network regarding his derogatory remarks, but never got an apology reply or even an acknowledgement for the chef's crude and indecent comments. It is one thing to say that I do not know how to cook vegetarian food, and there is no shame in telling the truth. But it is completely different thing to say vegetarian food is disgusting. My mom's opinion of him completely changed and is no more an idol to her. That great chef lost the admiration of my mom, and that one event debased his character and demeaned his reputation.

"Everything went as usual after that incident, except that my mom stopped watching any of the chef's shows. He lost all the respect that my mom had for him. She grew antipathy towards him. A year or so went by, and one day, after our typical fabulous dinner, my mom told us that what we just ate was all vegetarian. In fact, what we were eating for the past year or so was all vegetarian. Everyone in my family were utterly aghast as we falsely thought that vegetarian dishes would be tasteless and insipid.

"There were of course some dishes that were made to look like meat because the vegetables were quite obvious, but we were completely awestruck and astounded when we heard that revelation. For some reason, I was captivated by that discovery and asked my mom how it was possible. She told me a fable:

"Long time ago, a king, and a few of his soldiers, went deep into the woods on a hunting expedition. Though they all held together and vigilantly wandered around in the forest, the king regrettably got separated from others. Riding aimlessly on his horse, he found a small cottage near a riverbank. An old woman was inside the hut, and being hungry, the king beseeched if he could have some food. Despite being impoverished and destitute, the old woman couldn't say no to a hungry man at her doorstep. So she went out, chipped some grass clippings, and prepared the king some food with grass. The king gulped and relished the food with great gusto. Soon after, the soldiers also found the chalet and reunited with the king. It was then, the old woman found out that the person begging for food was the king. Just before they were about to leave, the king ordered his soldiers to find out the recipe for the delicious food and convey it to the royal chefs. Fearful of retribution, the old lady omitted mention of the core ingredient: grass.

"After the king was back to his palace, he asked his royal chefs to prepare the same dish he ate in the woodland. The royal cooks tried several times exactly as they were told, but the king was displeased as they couldn't get the dish taste anywhere near the flavor he savored back in the woods. Disappointed, the king later summoned the old lady to the palace to cook the dish. Assuming the king would punish her for serving him food made from grass, she got scared and tried to prepare a dish from other ingredients, but she couldn't get it anywhere close to the taste of the original dish. As she continued trying other dishes, it got past king's lunchtime and he started to get angry and petulant. The lady, seeing the king becoming vexed and irked, finally decided to concede the consequences of her misdemeanor, prepared the dish with grass clippings, and served him. The king, now famished, relishes the dish, exalts the woman and bestows her with several gifts. But just before the lady was about to leave the palace, the king felt he had to ask the secret ingredient. With apprehension, the woman disclosed that she served him grass. The king, who was delighted and in high spirits until he found out that he ate grass, precipitously started to berate her, and as a punishment, the old woman was imprisoned."

"Though my mom told the story in a convincing way, I knew it was a fantasy, an apocryphal story which she could have manipulated because of her bias and beliefs. But before I could suspect that she was taking advantage of my naivety and credulity, I found myself incredulous when I discovered that the steak I thought I ate for dinner that day was in fact eggplant. It was then became clear to me that the taste lies not in the tongue, but in the mind.

"We continued to have only vegetarian food in our home and never regretted that we stopped eating meat. I slowly started learning how to cook from my mom. By the end of my high school, I had developed a deep passion for cooking. I got into cooking so much that my wish list for Christmas and birthday gifts included skillets and frying pans, baking cups and bowls, food mixers and blenders. I loved every moment I spent in the kitchen with my mom and would proudly come out of kitchen with an exhilarated feeling that I made those delectable and savory dishes with my own two hands.

"Ever since I became fond of cooking and realized my passion for it, I wanted to turn it into a career. But as I found out, many chefs hate cooking vegetarian dishes and there weren't many professional vegetarian chefs. Still, I became determined to become a chef, exclusively a vegetarian chef. One day, during the last year in high school, I summoned up my courage and told my parents that I didn't want to go to college and instead wanted to completely concentrate on my goal of becoming a professional chef. My parents were not receptive to the idea. They got worried about my future and somehow convinced me to do a bachelor's degree in nutrition while I train as chef.

"Though there are several vegetarian culinary schools, I decided to train under my mother's mentorship. She is not a professional chef, but if my mom could serve us vegetarian food every day for about a year without us realizing we were not eating meat, I decided that there is no better professional training I could get other than emulating and mastering my mom's dishes. Eventually her recipes and techniques became sacrosanct to me and I adhered to them religiously.

"I trained under my mom all throughout the college while getting my degree. The knowledge and skills, theories and techniques my mom taught became the building blocks for me to explore cooking that suits any diet or any style of vegetarianism. We went to several food festivals to get feedback on our dishes and also prepared food for catering for special events.

"After college, our family had to move as my father got a new job in Philadelphia. And with encouragement and support from my father, my mom and I decided to open a vegetarian restaurant. We knew it would be a hard battle and we'd be working against the odds because Philadelphia tops the list of U.S. cities with the heaviest meat consumption. But we were pretty confident that we could do good business in the meat lovers city because our vegetarian dishes taste quite good, and any connoisseur of food would attest that our food is on par, or better than any Philly cheesesteak.

"But I couldn't get a bank loan as I have nothing to put as collateral. So, my dad provided the initial capital investment from his savings. I was single then and working eighteen hours a day to get the restaurant going. I didn't have time for myself, but I was okay with that. Both my mom and I were physically and mentally prepared as we knew it would be a hard and challenging battle. After about six months of hard work, we finally opened our restaurant 'AahhaaR' in early 2019.

"Though the initial influx of customers was very high, it slowly went to a steady state level, a level that was measurably unsustainable. A few years ago, we were struggling and enduring hardship running the restaurant. It was around that time, Audi visited my restaurant. I was flabbergasted to see Audi, the CEO of a mega-corporation, coming to my restaurant to eat. I didn't even know that Audi was a gourmand. I asked her if she had completely turned vegetarian or if she was just trying it out. She told me that by the end of our high school, as her conscience evolved, she decided to become vegetarian.

"We chatted for a while, during which time I mentioned that I am having a hard time running the restaurant business in Philadelphia and hinted I should move to a city with more vegetarian eaters. I also told her that we had tried a lot of incentive programs such as half-price lunches and free appetizers with dinner, but none of them worked. Audi boosted my confidence and told me that instead of fleeing from the problem, I must take it as a challenge and to start to think outside the box. She said, 'Your food tastes really great and should actually make meat eaters envy. So, find out *why* people are not flocking to your restaurant, rather than *what* you can do to attract more customers. You are in the right market. There aren't many vegetarian restaurants in the city. So, you must be missing something. Find out what that is.'"

Just as Radha was about to reveal what she did after Audi's advice, Audi was back from her phone call and joined us. She apologized for her absence, and told us that she made a commitment to herself to be always available to her employees.

"There's no need to be sorry," I said. "Being the head of a company comes with a lot of responsibility." Audi smiled magnanimously at me. I took her hand. "You know, Audi," I started slowly, "I must sincerely compliment you. I've heard a lot about your leadership skills today and I am very impressed." She hugged me in her Audi way, and squeezed my hand, thankful for the kind words as though she didn't hear them all the time.

There were a couple of things I'd been wanting to ask her, and I felt that was as good a time as any. Although it felt a bit like an interview, I boldly ventured in, knowing Audi was always ripe for conversation about these kinds of things. I turned towards her and put on my interview face. "So, I have two questions," I said, smiling. "I know you code, but I have been longing to know how you got into computer programming? The second question is, I want to know the secret behind how you're able to lead your company as not just a boss, but a leader who's crafted an exceptional culture?"

Audi tucked a piece of hair behind her ear, looking thoughtful as she spoke. "Well, things changed after that birthday when my dad gave me the laptop as a gift. You remember: both my mom and dad are office employees and very industrious, so their work demanded them working almost twelve hours a day, every day. Though it was stressful at times, they loved the work they did. When I was young, I resented that they chose work instead of playing with me. But when I got into teens and began to think on my own, I realized that raising our big family was a plow drawn with my mom and dad yoking together and working very hard. And if they could not spend much time with me, I decided that I could spend time with them by helping them out with their work. So I started doing data entry tasks for my dad on my laptop.

"Though the laptop was a gift, I wanted to earn a return on it. So, every day after school work, I reduced my TV time to learn how to write and debug computer programs. It took me few weeks to realize that coding is like hot liquid metal that can be molded into any shape, size, and form, and that it is a creative art. I spent the summer of 2011 learning different computer languages. As you may recall, it was the time the smartphones were getting bigger and starting to appear in diverse sizes, and many businesses were struggling to make their websites compatible for both phones and laptops. With my newfound interest in coding, I created a website for the capitals of states and countries, and I made the GUI compatible with any device. I submitted my flexible code and the website for the media class project that year. As a result, I was selected as one of the students to represent our school at the state level media science contest that year.

"Although I didn't win any scholarship, I got a colossal opportunity to network with many sponsors and understand the breadth of coding. I understood how everyone has different requirements for coding and the need for my code to be highly fluid and flexible. I made it my style and signature to always code in such a way that it is highly adaptable. Being able to attend the competition was by itself a great return, but I also won a consolation prize of $500 and earned a return on the laptop. I later continued to attend free workshops on coding and kept on participating in various contests. Personally, I never won any competition or coding scholarships, but I earned the zeal to better myself. My goal was simply to get better than yesterday.

Audi quickly moved on to answering my second question without giving me time to reflect on what she said in response to my first one. "Regarding SYMBIOSIS's culture," Audi continued, "when I was about to start my company ten years ago, I was very well prepared for everything, but at the same time I was a bit scared as I'd never run an enterprise before. I had never had people working for me. So, I went to my dad for advice. My dad told me, 'Over the years I have seen you transform into a leader. I have seen you acknowledge the limitations of your knowledge and accept the fact that you don't always have all the answers but are willing to ask questions and seek ways to creative problem solve. What more advice I can provide you?'

"I told my dad that I was afraid of how I would manage conflict resolution, provide guidance, and cultivate corporate ethics. My dad then told me a few leadership principles that I decided to follow 'til my last breath. He said, 'If you want to be remembered for your leadership in your employees' lives, care for them. Your employees are people, not objects. Acknowledge each person's uniqueness and their ideas. Appreciate them for their efforts, achievements, and triumphs. Your employees are giving their time, effort, and their life's purpose for you. So make sure their achievements and accomplishments belong to them. With your leadership, constantly fuel their creativity and curiosity, and promote a culture of innovation. You are their confidence and faith. Keep your promises and don't lose their trust and respect. Let your leadership character and effective management style speak for itself in building trust and discipline. Never compromise your integrity and honesty. And remember, as a leader, all successes belongs to your employees and all failures belong to you.'

"Every dime I have earned would not even begin to pay for the profound lesson I received that day. I make sure that there is always trust between employees and management with an honest, truthful, candid communication, and complete transparency. Our leadership understands that every employee has different insights into a problem and the creative process of problem solving, which can be contradictory and sometimes leading to discord. Instead of averting or resolving disharmony, we actually welcome it. The more ideas we hear, the more optimal and better solutions we can reach. We do have people from different backgrounds and expertise, and so conflicts will sometimes crop up. In such situations, we've trained our leadership to empathetically listen and understand each employee's problem without premature judgment so as to provide a win-win resolution."

I was completely wrapped up in Audi's comments, and when the doorbell rang, I nearly jumped. Audi excused herself and left the room. As I settled thinking the anecdote about the competition, I remembered Audi taking part in several competitions during high school, and my gang and I ridiculing her for not winning any of them. Wow, I thought, little did I know during my arrogant high school years that Audi was tasting success anyway, because she was setting her own goal and competing against that only. She totally redefined the definition of competition. While everyone else competed to win, Audi competed against herself and learned from other contestants.

At the same time, I could not escape the sense that I was discovering the qualities and hallmarks of a true leader. A leader understands that they do not have all the right answers all the time and they do not hesitate to show vulnerability. A leader also understands that they will never reach creative solutions if they obdurately hold on to being "right", or adamant and headstrong that they know everything.

In fact, a leader is receptive to both receiving and giving criticism as they know that criticism is an integral part of creativity. A leader sincerely apologies if someone is hurt, appreciates that each person is unique, and takes true accountability for their actions. I was seeing a true leader in Audi. I learned that a leader sees undiscovered, latent potential in every person and inspires to unleash that dormant creativity and talent. With their obsession for innovation and as an engine of growth, a leader encourages others to do something new and take risks. With no room for hypocrisy, they sincerely make limitless contribution to others' growth, not to their own ego.

Leaders understand that they are not omniscient and are willing to humbly educate themselves daily as lifelong learners. They always see a capacity to grow and they never stop challenging themselves. Their mindset remains the same no matter how much gratification, accolades, kudos and eminence they received from past accomplishments, as they always think that the most crucial and valuable work they will ever do is ahead of them. And undoubtedly, the very moment a leader thinks they have accomplished everything they can and have reached the pinnacle of their career, they are intellectually dead from that moment.

As Audi followed her dad's advice to its core, she saw her role in the company similar to the role of a farmer who not only undertakes the responsibility to rigorously select the finest seed, but also takes up the burden of plowing and fertilizing the land, and later weeding out the negativity for the seed to burgeon and thrive. I had never seen where a few words of wisdom could have such a significant impact in anyone's life.

While I was thinking about the profound impact Audi's dad had on her, I remembered that Radha had not yet finished her story. I was craving to ask and anxious to learn what happened after Audi's visit. I curiously asked her if she discovered her *why*, and how her restaurant was doing.

Radha jumped right back into our conversation, deftly recalling exactly where she left off. "I decided to take Audi's advice and resolved to find out why people were not allured by my vegetarian dishes. I was sure that most people were wise enough to distinguish between the right and the wrong. I was also sure that most people have an aversion to killing animals for food due to their reverence for all life, because an honest introspection would decisively lead to the conclusion that animals are not products. So I felt there must be something else that kept them from eating vegetarian dishes. I wasn't wanting to completely transform everyone into vegetarians, but at least give vegetarian dishes a try. So, I decided to go around the city and ask everyone I met.

"Almost everyone I met understood the ethical concerns and the cruelty to the animals, but everyone was worried that by eating vegetarian or vegan diet they would not get enough protein and other nutrients in their diet and would later have health issues. What I realized then was that there was a general misconception that we need animal meat to meet the body's needs. But the truth is, there are a lot of excellent vegetarian and vegan protein-rich foods that have enough protein and nutrients in the daily diet to meet the body's needs. I learned then that lack of knowledge, awareness, or misinformation about nutritional facts was making many people fail to choose plant-based diets.

"With my background in nutrition, I decided to bring awareness to the public regarding nutritional info so that people can make prudent decisions. I wanted to change their assumptions and fundamentally change their thinking. I wasn't just interested in bringing in more customers to my restaurant. I felt a bigger calling.

"I wanted to educate and enlighten people and show that they have a better solution that doesn't have to feel like such a compromise. There are also obvious health benefits with vegetarian diet. So, I decided to dedicate my life to making a difference in the world by helping chefs educate their customers on nutritional information. To debunk the general belief about proteins, nutrition and animal meat, I started a newsletter called '*The Zealous Vegetarian*' and published five vegetarian and vegan cookbooks where we post nutritional comparisons between vegetarian and meat products so that the public can choose what is best for them.

"I have had many successes and failures over the years, but the greatest consolation I have is the abstention from flesh and that I haven't eaten meat for the last eighteen years."

Before I could compliment her, Radha looked towards the kitchen. "Excuse me," she said, pointing to where her eyes fell. "I have to go finish dinner. Also, I can't recall whether I kept the chocolate pudding in the refrigerator. Have to make sure it coagulates!" She smiled, walking off.

As she disappeared around the corner, Ethan and Abi walked in.

As we chatted while awaiting Radha's dinner, I knew I was going to hear some shocking revelations, but I was definitely not prepared for the bombshell surprise that Abi was married to Adam, the star of now-defunct but widely popular and torrid pop band. I was expecting Ethan's wife, Sydney, to also join us, especially given that she is just a few weeks away from delivery. With no sight of Sydney, I chided Ethan how could he leave an eight-month pregnant woman alone at home. Abi swiftly interjected and said, "Sydney is the strongest girl I ever met in my life. She is both physically and emotionally hardy and resilient. If you think Audi is emotionally rugged, Sydney is several-fold tougher than Audi." Abi continued in her typical humorous tone, "And you know what, Sydney, now at full blown pregnancy and at the nadir of her physical stamina, can do more push-ups than Ethan could do during the zenith of his prime."

Abi is such an extraordinarily multi-talented person that she usually doesn't praise anyone. But for her to exalt someone, and especially comparing to Audi whom I thought is the strongest person I ever knew, it piqued my interest and I grew extremely curious to know about Ethan's spouse Sydney. I asked Ethan to tell me more about her.

SYDNEY

Ethan took a breath. "Sydney comes from a family of veterans," he said with a proud look, "and all she ever wanted from childhood was to serve people and our country. At twelve years old, she decided she would join the Navy and defend our country. She focused on her goal and worked very hard for it. Her family also supported her, helping her to train well both physically and mentally. During high school, she applied both to the Navy and to colleges. She got offers from both. Instead of enrolling in a college, she decided to pursue her dream of serving the country. She's a year younger than us, and she started her Navy career in late 2015, after graduating from high school. It was everything she ever wanted.

"But while reverently serving in the Navy, the unending and horrendous news of all the atrocious mass shootings in our country started to sicken her. Particularly because the lunatic culprits of those heinous crimes were not foreigners. They were American citizens. She started questioning if she was in the right battle, fighting for the right cause. While she was introspecting and interrogating herself, in November 2019, just before Thanksgiving break, she heard the gruesome news of a mass shooting at a high school in Chicago. But this time the harrowing news struck her direct and deep. Sydney lost her dearest family member, her younger sister Courtney.

"Sydney rushed to the hospital as soon as she landed at the airport, but before she could arrive, Courtney was pronounced dead. Sydney struck me one time when she said that her cute little sister who aspired to become a doctor was examined by a doctor, who counted the number of bullets she took."

I looked up to see everyone listening. Although I was certain everyone else already knew the story, it seemed as though they were hearing it for the first time. Tears glistened in everyone's eyes. I guess it's better you never get used to hearing something so sad.

"Courtney took bullets that were intended for her friends. From the recounts of fellow students, Sydney learned about the bravery of her intrepid sister and her courage to stand before the fear of death while helping her classmates run for their life. Sydney saw not only a true American, but a human that day. She couldn't be prouder of her sister. But at the same time, she realized that it wasn't just her sister that she buried, but also the hope and belief of a teenager that their country was the best place to live. After that cataclysmic loss, Sydney became convinced that she'd made a wrong decision in her life.

"When Sydney joined the Navy, she took an oath to protect the people from any outside threats. On one hand, there are countries that may try to harm us, and we have brave soldiers who put their lives up as an impregnable wall for safety of all the people. On the other hand, there are maniacs who are born and brought up in the same culture as we are and who try to hurt our fellow citizens. There is no justification for such lunatic actions. It is not right to test the power of their guns and the magnitude of their madness on innocent and unarmed civilians. Sydney no longer felt the threat from outside enemies and concluded that she was fighting the wrong battle. She saw a greater threat of enemies within the country and saw no point in serving at the border when the people within the country are dying of hate crimes. She saw no point in protecting a country of dead people."

At Abi's prodding, Ethan pulled out his phone to show us all the video clip of Courtney's funeral. Ethan's family had also attended Courtney's funeral, which was telecast on the local news channels. The memorial service was attended by several heads of state. After a dirge and the solemn knell, the video showed Sydney walking towards the podium with her head down. She took a note from her pocket and started reading the eulogy she had written for her sister.

"Dear Courtney,
Here's what you should have done.
You should have been in a safe place,
No, wait! You were inside a school building.
You should have called for help,

No, wait! Your teachers needed protection too.
You should have asked your friends for help,
No, wait! You saw them die in front of you.
You should have run for your life,
No, wait! A bullet travels faster than you.
You should have at the very least tried convincing the gun,
No, wait! Guns have no emotions.

Should I be happy or sad that you are in a better and safe place now?
Should I be happy or sad that you are in everyone's thoughts and prayers now?
Should I be happy or sad that you left this festered world, and no one can harm you now?
Should I be happy or sad that you deserted me, but you are not alone now?

I'm sorry we failed you.
I'm sorry school couldn't keep you safe.
I'm sorry we couldn't protect you.
I'm sorry you needed protection around your own people.
I'm sorry that sadly you are not the first, and unfortunately will not be the last, to sacrifice your life to satisfy the ego of a psycho.
I'm sorry that no punitive measures would befittingly serve the criminal for what he did to you and your friends.
I'm sorry that smart people will come up with a long list of reasons that led to shooting, but guns will never bear the blame.
I'm sorry that there will be a few upholding that the criminal was mentally unstable.
I'm sorry that we take pride in fighting for our age old Constitution above saving people's lives.
I'm sorry that we live in a country where the gun laws take precedence over the right to live.
I'm sorry that our government will soon find a distraction before providing a proper solution.
I'm sorry that intelligent solutions will end up fighting violence with violence.
I'm sorry that you will be a topic of discussion for few days followed by an echo of dead silence until the next tragedy.
I'm sorry that we can only tell you sorry. Again, and again, I'm sorry. I'm sorry.

With regrets and hopelessness, your sister, Sydney."

But Sydney didn't just stop there with the elegy. She raised her head and faced the congregation, the look in her eyes intense. Every person has a breaking point and at that critical moment of adversity, one naturally and spontaneously gets inborn courage. Even a lamb roars like a lion if cornered. With the sudden catastrophic loss of her little sister, Sydney experienced that turning point but didn't lose her control. Instead, with equanimity and displaying utmost social propriety, she politely took a stab at the lawmakers with some gut-wrenching and thought-provoking questions. She made them stand naked in their ignorance towards the problem.

Continuing her address, she said, "Esteemed dignitaries, thank you for making time to come here today and standing with us in our rough times of trials and tribulations. We received your thoughts and prayers, and we are working hard to send them towards our lost ones. With your permission I would like to speak to you. I have some questions for you to discuss during your roundtable conferences.

"There may be a lot of things that went wrong with the processes and checks that resulted in this misfortune that has dawned upon us, but let me ask you this: When you see a toddler reaching for, or holding a kitchen knife, what would your acute response be? Would you calmly take away the knife and make sure they will never be able to reach it again, or would you educate the child in the hopes that they will never attempt to grab it again? Courts and lawmakers are still flummoxed with the language and the meaning of our second amendment. So, explaining to a teenager, or even an adult, the right to a gun by invoking the second amendment is similar to elucidating a toddler why we have a knife in the home.

"A gun may be a right to protect in this country, but it is clearly being misused. Guns have become a leisurely route for personal vendetta and for becoming notoriously famous, and this must stop as it is past time we follow 'live and let live'. The answer for violence is not violence. The solution for a gun is not another gun. The function of the government should be to change the society such that we don't want and don't need guns.

"Try to first attack the source of the problem, not the superficial reasons. Suppose you walk out of your bedroom one morning or enter your home after a week-long vacation and find out that your home reeks with the noisome stench of rotten garbage in your kitchen that you forgot to dispose of. What would you do? Would you first remove and discard

55

the source of pungent odor, and then spray an air freshener, or do you continue to treat your home with malodor neutralizer to cover-up the fetid odors without removing the source? We are collectively asking you to do what you would do in such a situation. I hope you are wise enough to comprehend my analogy. Majority of the people in our society do not want what you think that they want, and I hope you are educated and intelligent enough to discern that.

"I stand here not to grieve about our loss today. Instead, I stand here today to pledge that no more lives will be interrupted this way. No student should be afraid to go to school. No teacher should hold a gun instead of a pen. No school should smell blood instead of flowers. Having guns is a constant reminder that we live in fear. Great minds who came before us already proved that 'only a coward needs a gun'. So when you are done with your prayers, I hope you will actively engage in dealing with the root of the problem. Remember, life is more precious than a law."

I have attended many funerals in my life and witnessed many people reciting maudlin and mawkish poems for their elegy, but never in my life had I heard such an introspective lament.

After we watched the painful yet thoughtful speech, which was neither a tirade nor a harangue, Ethan continued with his story. "Sydney didn't expect those brilliant minds which came up with completely unrelated list of reasons and adamantly stupid conclusions for that tragedy would be able to open their eyes and abjure their beliefs on the source of the problems in this country, but she waited. She wanted that event to be the last school shooting in United States history and end the epidemic of school violence. She wanted a permanent change of the law and advocated gun reform. During that waiting time, Sydney and student groups tirelessly organized several gun control rallies in all major cities in US calling for tighter gun laws. Their calls for gun control were not different to those in the aftermath of other tragedies. However, the magnitude and ferocity of the public in response to deadliest of such atrocities had given a lot of hope and led many people to believe that this time felt different. News and social media became tools to promulgate awareness, and thousands of supporters of all ages, from strollers to walkers, participated in the marches and voiced their rights and demands.

"In the end, all that Sydney received from government officials was 'thoughts and prayers', and the insistence they too deplored the sickening behavior of the reprobate murderer. Though Sydney never accused the government of abdicating its responsibilities, she acknowledged that they seemed useless in the gun issue as some politicians kept quiet and others shunned the protesters. Some politicians made it a completely different issue, one with nothing to do with safety. Some alleged that it was a mental health issue, but Sydney understood it to be far more than that. We have a gun problem. Some just asserted that it was a terrible tragedy and that it should never have happened. And some callous people, without any shame, defended gun associations with no appreciation for life. After all, politics is a game of advantage. There was no earnest will or policies to actively protect the schools. Guns have transformed, evolved and upgraded at an incredible rate, but our laws have not. As Sydney found out, while other developed countries have enacted gun safety laws, our country developed websites to report and summarize mass shootings for statistics. Our Second Amendment allows guns, but in and around schools should be one of the places where guns should not be allowed. And if nothing is done to actively block guns near the schools, students will continue to die and add to the statistics. Though politicians acknowledge that, those sanctimonious hypocrites lacked the compassion to act.

"The response from our leaders that nothing could have been done to forestall and preclude these shootings did not appease Sydney. She knew that they were blatantly lying. It was obvious. She even questioned if the leaders were mentally ill. Even children understand that guns are dangerous, and schools are no place for them. After a few months on standby, it became evident that Sydney tried to enlighten stubbornly foolish and rigidly idiotic elected officials, and that she herself needed to do something. She could no longer endure inaction from government officials.

"Though disaffected, she didn't feel powerless. She decided to give up her Navy career and become a police officer trained to handle active shooter situations. She joined a team tasked to secure and protect schools and public places from violent and hateful crimes. During that time, Sydney saw billions of dollars being spent on high-tech security of the schools such as metal detectors at entrances, bulletproof safe rooms and panic buttons in each classroom, gunshot detection sensors and security cameras in hallways, impenetrable classroom doors, the list went on and on.

"More security and high-tech products in schools was thought to work, but they didn't; attacks became routine and people started to become inured to the horrific news of shooting deaths. Metal detectors unfortunately only detected, and their location at the entrances made them already too late to stop a maniac entering the school with a semi-automatic weapon. Safe rooms and panic buttons became ceaseless reminders for students that they were living in fear and only instilled more terror, making the students jaded and feel like they were under constant siege.

"As a cop, though she did her duty well, she was not satisfied. As school shootings continued to become frequent news, her faith in humanity was sorely tested. She felt powerless in obviating the crime. While she kept asking intriguing questions such as, 'Why do some people commit violence?', 'When did they turn into a misanthrope?' and 'How could they justify their actions?', she found out that those people do not see any other alternatives and are ready to accept the consequences of their violent act. She then realized that she was fighting the crime the wrong way. After working for a year as a police officer, in early 2021, she left the police force and started a non-profit organization going into schools and public meetings trying to advance ways to fight crime with a motto that country cannot be built unless people learn to be united and have love and respect for fellow beings.

"Seeing children spending their time in dread and trepidation on the school premises, Sydney concluded that safety and security should start from outside the school. She noticed that not all schools have closed-circuit cameras outside the buildings or in the parking lots. She educated the school management on the importance and value of having cameras around the premises and in the parking lots. But when schools responded that they had insufficient funds to augment the exterior infrastructure, it saddened her. She decided to raise the funds to buy the equipment integral to keep the schools safe. Having gained the trust and approbation, Sydney's biggest support came from parents and the school management. They stood together to protect the children. While some parents dug into their savings, others went door-to-door raising money. Sydney also met with almost every company in town, big and small, who could help sponsor the necessary equipment. Few helped, and many didn't.

"Sydney continued that quest to install cameras outside the schools for about a year until January of 2022. But eventually she realized that having mere cameras and metal detectors would not solve the problem. She concluded that we needed a better early warning system, an active vigilance system. She was looking for a discreet weapon-sensing device which scans in real-time without forcing students to line up or walk through the metal detectors. She wanted it to be simple, clean and obscure, so people wouldn't even consciously realize it was there.

"During that hunt, Sydney asked me if I knew of any such dynamic real-time surveillance system. I told her we could build one. Sydney then quickly moved from Chicago to Phoenix to help develop the system."

Typical of Ethan, he explained the system, though I understood very little of what he said. "To come up with such an inconspicuous setup, Audi and I decided to combine the sensor technologies we were developing at **SYMBIOSIS** and seamlessly integrate into the existing cameras outside the schools. As a result, we developed a camera that rotates once every two seconds on a vertical axis and takes high resolution overlapping images up to 100 yards distance in the ultraviolet, visible, and infrared wavelengths of the electromagnetic spectrum. The image data is then first run through an algorithm to produce a 3D model with the distances to the objects and the structures, similar to the **LIDAR** sensor system used in aerial surveillance or obstacle detection for autonomous cars. If the computer detects any suspicious structures, like the shape of a gun or a knife, then the image is run through machine learning algorithms to reduce false positives and also simultaneously fed into hyperspectral image processor to analyze the composition of the structure to differentiate between a toy gun vs. real gun, plastic knife vs. metal knife, or real human vs. mannequin. We then added a little spice of artificial intelligence and superfast algorithms to the system to survey, detect, and secure in real-time.

"Of course, no technology is perfect and even with our latest machine-learning algorithms which can distinguish much better, we still get some false positives to this day, though they have exponentially reduced from the day we introduced this system in the schools. But false positives are taken very sportively, and no one, either the school system or the students oppose for inspection because it is better to be safe than sorry. If any student or a person was tagged as carrying harmful objects and later found out that it is a false positive, they are well compensated with a gift card paid by our company.

"And again, with the colossal support from parents and generous donations, Sydney retrofitted the existing cameras with the new sensors in every school. The schools have become safer these days with the novel use of the sensor technology. All the schools across the country are now safer, and the unwarranted and gratuitous gun violence inside or around the schools has significantly reduced over the years. As you probably know, this is the third consecutive year without any shooting inside any school across the country. While half the credit goes to Sydney, the other half goes to Audi for suggesting creative ideas and supporting us at every step of our failures."

Though Sydney's story started with a tragic loss and we all empathized with her situation as evinced by tears in everyone's eyes at one point, I got very interested to find out how she pulled herself out of it and found a new purpose in life. Ethan's narrative of Sydney's past clearly showed her guiding motto in life: If something smells bad, make it a duty to fragrance it. Though Sydney wasn't there with us, we all applauded her unwavering and indefatigable efforts. Her story clearly is an example that no selfless deed goes unrecognized. Those technological achievements materialized not because of an affluent person, but by an ordinary person with unselfish passion and noble vision. Moreover, what astounded me was, whatever the life threw at her and whichever direction she was oriented, she was able to quickly adapt to the change, circumvent every bad situation, and always found a way to serve the country and its people.

The time was about 7:40 pm and I was starting to feel hungry. And just in time, Radha announced the dinner was ready. After hearing Radha's story, I was zealously waiting to taste her vegetarian dishes. Ethan proposed we all sit in the family room and eat while watching a movie. Abi proposed a better plan: Instead of a movie, we should look at our prom pictures.

After a while, it became clear that it was impossible to reach a unanimous decision and like puerile teenagers, Ethan and Abi had to fight like feral cats to reach an agreement. Audi pulled out her archaic laptop, the same one she received as gift from her father for her fifteenth birthday. She always carried the laptop during our college days and I couldn't believe that she still had it after almost eighteen years. Even more remarkable was that it was in working condition. I was sure Audi refurbished the internal of the laptop with the latest technology. She made few clicks on the laptop, loaded Ethan's and Abi's voice profiles to her system and shouted, "Projector ON." The room started to shape-shift, the wall becoming a screen and what I thought was an ordinary ceiling fan became an in-built projector.

Ethan and Abi started their battle to test the amplitude of their arguments. Their fight reminded me the occasions in which I had similar arguments with Ethan. Ultimately, Abi won the duel and prom pictures were displayed. I expected the outcome. But what was startling to me was that Audi had all of our prom pictures. The last person I thought would have saved pictures from fifteen years ago was Audi.

Abi was the head of the student advisory board and she selected a big ballroom for prom night. Our theme was 'United World Fun,' where the idea was that each girl must represent a country of her choice. Abi, being half-Indian, chose India as she loves the designs on the saris they make. Her mother bought a scintillating handmade sari from India and Abi looked resplendent wearing it. Audi chose Japan and wore a kimono. Tanya went with sarafan, a Russian traditional dress. Clarisse chose an Italian traditional dress. I chose England and wore the famous princess gown topped with a hat.

As we kept glancing at the pictures, I grew slightly jealous of Audi. Her date for prom was Ethan. But that was my fault, a direct result of my narrow-mindedness. Ethan had a crush on me and asked me first to be his date, but I rejected him. Ethan later asked Audi and she agreed. And as I recall, the only reason I said no to him, my best friend, was because he wasn't a prepossessing sight. Instead I went with Kevin, who was ravishingly handsome. Kevin borrowed our math teacher's car and very politely asked for my parents' permission. My parents were nervous about me going to the prom, but after talking to Kevin, whom they trusted, they were relieved.

Pictures are a great way to restore memories. Every photo we saw had a story. It took us more than two hours to have our dinner as we stopped at each picture and talked about it. I was having a splendid time with my friends and I realized how much I missed them. I remember reading a post online that read something like, "True friends can go not talking for years and when they meet again, can still pick up just where they left off." It was absolutely true in our case and I felt that affinity sitting among my beautiful friends.

Radha's vegetarian meal was delicious and nutritious. After tasting the dishes, even the last grain of doubt I had in my mind had completely vanished. However, I also simultaneously questioned if it was my novelty to the cuisine that made it a pleasure. Topping off the main course, Radha served the best congealed chocolate pudding. The confection was yummy and lustrous. And as I found out, the secret ingredients in that delectable pudding were desiccated coconut flakes and cashew cream. After the sumptuous meal, we all sat comfortably in a torpid state and started to reminiscence those golden days and the fun times we had together. We lost track of the time and hoped it stood still so that we could keep talking. After a while, Ethan got a message on his phone which made us realize that it was past 11PM. So we decided to call it a night and meet at next day's reunion. With a wistful yearning for those glorious high school days, I was on my way back to the hotel room and all I could consciously ruminate was only about Audi.

Audi never cared about what others thought of her. During our high school and in college, she wore the same dress repeatedly every other day. She never followed the social mores and norms like blue is for boys and pink is for girls. I made fun of her when she wore her brother's blue socks to school. There were also several occasions where the color of both socks did not match. I wasted my time teasing and bullying her, but she never cared about that. Impervious to ridicule, Audi spent her valuable time concentrating on her goals.

I, on the other hand, acutely infected with Attendance Deficit Disorder, was one of the popular girls in high school. An artisan in the art of copying, I was not doing homework on my own. I was also tainted with traits of talking too much and making acerbic comments behind someone's back on their physical appearance, cracking mean jokes, creating and propagating a calumny, and much more. Among those ill-mannered traits, bullying my peers was my specialty trait. I was like a bloodhound with eyes of a dragonfly. No emotion was imperceptible to my senses. I could smell and spot the shy ones, the brainy ones, and also fear, insecurity and inferiority complex. I felt some joy and delight when I teased, ragged on and affronted my fellow classmates, but gained nothing else from it. But by laughing at others' expense, I definitely lost my dignity and decency, which I didn't realize then. Now that I think about it, it is still an unfathomable mystery to me as to how I felt amused by humiliating my fellow students, and why I felt delighted by tripping and throwing stuff at my friends. What I felt as a sense of upper hand on my classmates was in fact a symbol of my foolishness.

I felt no compunction, not even one time, when I thought about the repercussions of my corrosive behavior and the emotional pain I put my friends through. As I reflect on my classmates whom I bullied went through, it gives me deep regret and sorrow, and makes me feel ashamed to be a part of their list of bitter childhood memories. I derided my friends and made caustic comments on the types of clothes they wore, their hair styles, their nail polish, and many other trivial things. I hectored Audi for the dresses she wore, though I knew Audi never cared about apparel and make-up. I guess people bully for two main reasons - some do it as a defensive means because they are jealous of the person they are bullying and hence to eventually boost their self-esteem and overcome their shortcomings; some do it as a judgmental means to show their superiority and get noticed to gain and maintain popularity and a social status. As for me, for being felt inferior to Audi and Abi, and to preserve my status as the head of my gang, the contagion of bullying had poisoned me from both angles. Regardless of the reason, bullying is inordinately dangerous and an emotional equivalent to physically beating up someone. Unfortunately, there is nothing that I can do now to make it right but wholeheartedly apologize and ask for forgiveness.

Every one of us carries a dictionary composed of our beliefs and attitudes, but the doctrine that Audi carries has all the foolish words missing in it, and 'ominous' is one of those missing words. Audi considers that everything happening in her life is resulting in actually advancing her goals, even if the obstacles are setting her back. She regards the barriers, challenges, and even disappointments and disasters as a learning experience and an opportunity to evolve and grow.

One such debacle that Audi acknowledged and welcomed as an opportunity happened during the summer of 2016, after our second year in college. Ethan and Audi, along with a bunch of other students, applied for a summer internship in a sensor manufacturing company. It was the time when the prospecting technologies needed for autonomous vehicles and space exploration were being developed and tested. A tech company which was into manufacturing imaging sensors had advertised several positions for a three-month paid internship for the entire duration of summer break. Though some students applied just for the sake of money, Audi and Ethan applied for a learning experience. They wanted to learn how the three-dimensional images are obtained, how to reconstruct and develop software to digitally peel the outer layers from the images to visualize the internal composition of the scanned object, and how to perform a 3-D rendering of the imaged object for further analysis.

What was originally publicized as a learning experience turned out to be dud. Instead of taking the interns to the design and development facility, they were taken to the packaging facility for a dead-end monotonous job in a huge building with conveyor belts all over the place. And their task was to manually check the sensors that were riding the conveyor belts and package the ones that are good and throw away the ones that are bad. Dreary and dull as it sounds, everyone saw that task as a humdrum.

After every student left in the evening to spend the money they'd just earned, Ethan and Audi stayed back. Instead of throwing the inferior sensors out, they studied them. In their inquisitiveness, they learned the internal working of the sensor, what was causing the defect, and so much more that they would have not learned if the internship wasn't a bust. What other students thought of as their bad luck and misfortune to be selected for that internship, Ethan and Audi saw it as a boon and a tremendous opportunity to learn. When other students railed it as a depressing and a tedious job, Ethan and Audi complimented the internship as a productive launching pad, and as a remarkable experience.

Just as the maxim "beauty is in the eye of the beholder", every job is what we make of it, not what is delegated to us. It's all in our outlook and perspective. Just as one can commend and acclaim the good things about a tree-- that it gives us shade, oxygen, fruit, and an abode for birds-- one can also excoriate and chastise the same tree as spewing pollen resulting in severe allergies, and dusting away dead leaves all over in the fall season. It is all in our attitude, our outlook and perspective, if we see a rose bush with thorns or a thorn bush with roses.

With commingled thoughts, but with a deep sense of regret over my past bullying, I reached my hotel. I quickly checked my messages, notified my parents that I was back to my room safe, and got to bed.

KEVIN

In what must have been the result of the cumulative sleep deprivation of the last few days, the nature had imposed the preservative by inducing lethal sleep so much that I did not remember turning off my alarm. When I was finally woken up by my phone ringing, the yellow effulgent ball that we call 'Sun', was little high up in altitude and trying its best to pierce through the curtains. The phone call was Audi and Abi letting me know that they were thirty minutes away from picking me up for the reunion in Flagstaff, Arizona. Realizing I overslept, I rushed to the bathroom and started multitasking like a circus clown.

Radha had left to head to the reunion early that morning, so it was only Audi, Abi and me in Audi's autonomous car. The first thing I did that morning was to genuinely apologize for my atrocious bullying during our high school. Abi laughed it out and said she actually liked the name "Brainiac"; Audi just smiled and digressed the subject. Clearly, they had both moved on. But I was sure they were bothered initially when I started bullying them. Who wouldn't be? However, during the later years of high school, they just quietly ignored my teasing endeavors. It is a seemingly simple yet perfect solution, because every form of bullying is powerless without a reaction from the victim and them purposely disregarding my badgering naturally drove me to nuts.

On our way, we quickly visited a wildlife sanctuary in the national forest near Flagstaff that Audi started to protect and conserve endangered species before any vestige of their presence on Earth disappears forever. As quirky as Audi is, the sanctuary was also odd. While it is conventional for the wildlife be caged and barricaded, the visitors to that quixotic haven are put in a van resembling a cage and the wildlife was in their natural state. As the van drove on the tour's tortuous path, among other terrestrial animals I was thrilled to watch in that serene utopia, I spotted swarthy Asian elephants, nocturnal red pandas in their arboreal habitat, and a Bengal tiger couple with variegated stripes.

As we were short on time, we curtailed the sanctuary visit by cutting the trip to the aquatic park, and by about 11AM we reached the resort. With Abi around, we didn't realize the time during the drive. She can create humor from anything. Abi was looking at her phone and she quickly said, "He needs to go the gym before his hands gets lost in his face." We didn't know what she was talking about until she showed the phone and we all started laughing as she pointed at the hug emoji which showed only hands and the face. Abi had always been witty with impeccable comedic timing. She is so funny and clever that if for any reason the evolution had abruptly switched from the survival of the fittest to the survival of the wittiest, Abi is still on the top of the list.

Humor and satire are all about opportune timing and Abi has it. It was Abi's trenchant wit that broke the friendship-ending polemic between Ethan and me at the very end of our college days. It was April 2018, about a month from graduation, and Ethan and I started arguing about money. To Abi's bad luck, she stepped right into us while we were in the middle of a typhoon of debate. As I asked Abi to pick a side, she started a parody. Just a few days before, there was breakout news about a Facebook data scandal. Abi added a spin to the story and said, "Imagine if Google met Facebook a year ago. Facebook would say, 'I am sorry for your loss', and Google would say, 'It's okay. We knew it was going to happen as she had a lot of bugs.' But if they met now, Google would say, 'Well, at least she died knowing she didn't do anything wrong.'" I was puzzled at the spoof, but Ethan started laughing. Her mockery of Facebook and Google was not germane to the issue in question and was completely irrelevant to the fight, but she digressed the topic which somehow did the job of breaking up the fight. I did not understand, and though Abi reiterated the punchline, I still didn't get it. When I asked what the hell they were laughing about, they explained the oblique reference in the punch line. Abi was referring to Orkut, Google's version of Facebook, that Google had ended as it was losing its user base.

We reached Flagstaff. Compared to Phoenix, the weather was a bit chilly in Flagstaff, but it is nothing for a Chicagoan. As we entered the resort, a huge water fountain welcomed us. It was supposed to be one of the best resorts in town and it did please me well. We stepped down at a conveyor and saw the car slide into the parking. After the usual iris scan, we were escorted to our rooms. We were all allotted rooms on the same floor. The commodious room appeared to be aesthetically designed for the elite class and the list of amenities were probably concocted with an evil mind in such a way that the customers will become totally accustomed to and never will want to leave the hotel. As I pressed a remote to let in some natural light, I saw the blinds unfold to a visual spectacle of a beautiful natural cascade off the mountain side. While there were several comforts in the room in which I would partake, there were some features for which I didn't particularly see any use for, and one of them was an array of glass prisms installed at the window sill.

After dropping our stuff in our respective rooms, Audi, Abi and I walked down to the lobby and I saw Clarisse, one of the organizers of the reunion, checking in along with Kevin. In restless eagerness, I rushed to her to exchange a warm hug. Clarisse hadn't changed a bit; she looked the same, though she fiercely disagreed. But what boggled me and pleasantly surprised me was, the inarticulate, shy and stammered Clarisse married highly articulate, outgoing and impromptu speaking Kevin, my prom date. The two were poles apart in everything. Kevin is very lively, outspoken, and hosted all our school events, whereas Clarisse had glossophobia and wouldn't speak due to intense anxiety. They didn't have anything in common. I guess that's what made them a couple who complemented each other.

While we were in the lobby, in walked in Ethan and his beautiful wife. Abi's family was also arriving. As we were all introduced, I couldn't believe that I was meeting Adam from the once widely popular band Asher.

As we kept walking towards the ballroom, Ethan, Audi, Abi and Adam mysteriously got separated from us, and Sydney, Clarisse, Kevin and I got settled at one table. The first thing I did was offer Sydney my sincere condolences and reveal how I became a rabid fan of her overnight. However, I couldn't subdue my curiosity to know how Ethan and Sydney met and married. Sydney was very modest to my initial requests, but as I kept cajoling and begging for more details, she finally divulged more of their family life.

"Ethan is the best thing that ever happened to me," she said humbly. "He is my strongest pillar of support. My father and Ethan's father were very close high school friends. They both loved only three things in their life: the city of Chicago, aspiration to serve in the armed forces as soon as they were out of high school, and their respective high school sweethearts. As you probably know, Ethan's mom unexpectedly got pregnant while they were in the final year of high school. As a result, Ethan's dad had to relinquish his dream of serving the country. He helped Ethan's mom during the pregnancy and with the newborn, and they both finished high school. As Ethan's family stayed back, my dad got enlisted in the Army and had to move out of Chicago. We kept moving around depending on where my father got stationed. Eventually, when I was about ten years old, my family moved to Chicago and we stayed for three years before we had to move again. Ethan lost his father in a tragic accident while I was in Chicago in middle school. Though Ethan and I are family friends, I barely knew him during childhood as he was a very shy person. The most vivid recollection I have of him during my childhood is when he came to help us out during our relocation out of Chicago. After I joined the Navy, my dad retired from the Army and permanently took up residence in the city he loved the most.

"Several years later, I met Ethan by fortuity in a hospital during the Thanksgiving break of 2019. His mother wasn't feeling well for several months and they came in to corroborate the diagnosis. I didn't recognize his mom. I always remembered her smile and her spirited personality, but she looked different. She readily recognized me and consoled me on the tragic loss of my sister. I noticed Ethan standing next to his mom, holding her hand and listening to us talk.

"When his mom went to see the doctor, Ethan and I started talking. It was the first time we spoke after many years, and he asked how I was holding up. I always thought I was tough, but I couldn't control myself. With tears flowing like a waterfall, I broke into a mournful heaving sob. Though I nodded that I was okay, he knew I was in a precarious position. I usually do not confide in anyone outside my family, but for some reason I told Ethan that I was conflicted whether to continue in the Navy or not. Ethan handed in a tissue and said, 'You're a strong girl and our country needs a fighter like you. Do what you believe is right for the greater good.' Those words gave me the boost to make a decision.

"Soon, his mom came back from the doctor's office. She didn't say a word, but Ethan perceived that the doctor has confirmed the diagnosis. I saw his love for his mom in his eyes. As it is personal, I didn't want to ask what was wrong. But with his mom's permission, after my sister's funeral, he confided in me that his mom had been diagnosed with cancer and that he had decided to forsake his dreams of a Ph.D. and take up a job to pay for his mom's medical bills. He chose his love for his mom over his dream.

"I thought his future wife is the luckiest person on Earth because if he could adore his mom so much, how much would he compassionately care and cheerfully support his wife. A few days later, he graduated, moved to Phoenix to start working at SYMBIOSIS and was one of the first few to be hired by Audrianna. Around the same time, I left the Navy and started a new chapter in my life as a cop. His mom was still in Chicago, and Ethan was frequently shuttling between Phoenix and Chicago. We kept in constant touch, exchanging our opinions, and we met every time he flew to Chicago. It was a turbulent time in both our lives, and we found comfort in each other's company. Every time I felt debilitated, he would nurture mettle in me.

"A year later, his mom permanently moved to Phoenix and I started a non-profit organization. He had no reason to fly to Chicago anymore, but he would come frequently, and we would spend some time in each other's companionship. We never said 'I love you' to each other, but in our hearts we knew that we loved each other. About a year later, I was again feeling feeble and fragile. Ethan held my hand and made a promise that he would never let me feel powerless again and that he would become my fortitude. He asked me to move to Phoenix and I instantly did. Ethan and Audi later came up with the technology that revolutionized the way we look at school safety, and everything I have become, I owe it to them.

"Even with all the therapy, Ethan's mom's health slowly deteriorated. She knew her time on Earth was coming to an end. As a single mom, she raised Ethan and got him a good education. Like a candle consuming itself, she expended most of her adult life to give light to Ethan. But by seeing her vulnerable condition, Ethan would cry in helplessness. They both knew that there was no coming back from the last stage cancer. Though he had tears in his heart that he couldn't help or heal her, Ethan always kept her spirits high, even during her bedridden days.

"I grew up in the bosom of Armed Forces under the norm that men are supposed to be emotionally unbreakable. But seeing Ethan, I became cognizant that empathy, tenderness, and even crying actually ascribe to brave men, not to cowards.

"Ethan's mom had only two wishes left- that Ethan to get his Ph.D. and to see him marry before she died. While working at SYMBIOSIS, he enrolled in a part-time Ph.D. program, and about two and half years ago, in the summer of 2027, Ethan and I got married. Three months after, having battled cancer for more than eight years, his mom passed away, knowing in her heart that Ethan would eventually accomplish his ambition of a Ph.D."

Though Sydney had a strong southern dialect, I didn't have a hard time understanding her. Like Ethan, she was modest in recounting her story. She imputed the credit for all her great work to others and didn't take an ounce of credit for what she has achieved. But it did not thwart me from extolling her ideologies, decisions, and accomplishments.

I was happy that Ethan married the right person. The fact that they understood each other without articulately expressing is in fact true love, because true love is where you know the other person better than you know yourself. Their story is also a perfect example of the management principle of choosing first what is important, and within those important ones, choosing what is urgent, and within those urgent ones, choosing what is a priority for us. Sydney chose to leave the Navy as she believed that country will stand strong only if the people are stronger and united. Ethan chose to sacrifice his dream of higher studies to support the dream of bringing back his mother to health.

Either intentionally or inadvertently, Sydney made a point to tell me about Ethan crying. Ethan was very close to his mom. They were inseparable. Initially, he didn't want to go to Harvard because Boston being so far from Chicago and required him to leave his mom. But she somehow convinced him. Because of his relentless attacks of homesickness, I thought he was being a baby and excessively sentimental, which I also told him so. During our college days, Ethan used to go to Chicago, or his mom would visit Boston on every occasion they got.

I knew Ethan was not a conformist to the unwritten law of masculinity. But by openly disclosing that Ethan cried, Sydney broke a negative social and cultural stereotype, and a false generalization that men shouldn't emote, or be emotionally sensitive and easily susceptible simply because it is considered a form of weakness. Irrespective of the fact that the biology of the brains are different between men and women, in our society and culture, men are expected to squash their fear and pain. They are under immense social pressure to portray themselves as strong and invincible, and are taught that crying or expressing their softer feelings would make them look weak or otherwise fragile. For the same emotions, a woman might get a compassionate response and consoling comments while a man might get an advice to "man up". I wondered why this discrepancy in response for expressing the same feelings, and why a man and a woman is expected to react differently but in conformity to socially acceptable gender appropriate manner. I think it is okay for a man to cry. It is okay for a man to feel weak. These are basic human emotions. Having and emoting them makes us a better human. But of course, we need to be careful to use the right amount of emotions to make a balanced and delicious dish called 'Life'. Any overuse of one ingredient can ruin the dish all together.

Just then an obsequious waiter came distributing beer to our table. Clarisse and I fervently took a bottle each, and Sydney, being pregnant, declined. I noticed Kevin also rejected alcohol. So, I humorously asked him, "When are you due?" Kevin's reply to my old habit of ribbing completely surprised me. In a solemn tone, he said, "I have been a teetotaler all my life. And I don't intend to break my lifelong commitment to sobriety." He then excused himself to get some tea and met Ethan on his way.

Sometimes, we think we know everything about the person who sits in front of us or beside us in the classroom, but we really know nothing about that person even after spending months or years talking and working with them. That person for me was Kevin. All I knew about Kevin was that he was very bright, courteous, and charming as a delicately crafted, six-foot tall, irresistibly seductive wedding cake. He was a good friend and always used to tell us florid and turgid melodramas. But in reality, I didn't know anything about him or his family as I was never invited to his house. He also never celebrated his birthdays. Gripped by a gallant desire, I asked Clarisse to tell me more about Kevin. As Clarisse began to tell Kevin's traumatic childhood and how he overlooked and shunned the typical impulsive temptation, it had made me realize how tenacious and tender Kevin is.

"Kevin's mother had him at a very young age, when she was only sixteen years old. She didn't get any support from Kevin's father. Her family also deserted her. She became a single mother. As a teenager herself, still maturing and trying to raise a child without any support, she couldn't handle the pressure and gave up on school. She tried her best initially but couldn't handle the huge responsibility which she was not ready to take. To forget about her past and her mistakes, she started drinking her failures away with alcohol and cigarettes. She was never at home. With her meager means and unable to afford daycare, she started taking him wherever she went. She stole food and stood on the side of busy intersections with her newborn, begging for money. But whatever money she got, she spent on drinking and smoking.

"It didn't stop there. When Kevin was around five years old, he started noticing that strangers used to visit his home with his mother and it was a different man each night. One day, one of those strangers asked Kevin to accompany him to restroom. At that age, all Kevin could do was to protest and grumble to his mother about the man and the pain he felt. But all that Kevin's mother could say to him was that she was disgusted to even see his face and told him that she was generous enough to give him a roof to live under and that she never loved him. She told him that he is her dog and asked him to be one. That man also became a regular visitor until Kevin was eight years old, which is when Kevin stood tough and threatened the man to leave the house. He never saw that man again.

"Though Kevin's mother blamed him from childhood over what she perceived as failures and sorrows in her life, Kevin was born gifted, smart, sharp, and bright. Instead of providing him healthy support, she ragged and bullied him continually, and his job was to clean up after her. She never provided nutritious food; instead made him her personal bartender. Countless times Kevin had to forage for food and go dumpster diving. He spent most of his time in the school or at his neighbor's place. His local church provided him with used clothing that were donated. Anytime he wanted to show his mom how well he did or any awards he won, he felt like he was talking to a wall. His mom always found ways to remind him that he was unwanted, and that he ruined her life physically and mentally.

"He grew up with a mother who didn't care for him. He grew up seeing a new man every day with his mother. Inured to violence, he grew up emotionally abused by his mother and physically abused by the men who came for her in a hellish place that he called 'home'. Whenever she was depressed, she would scar him with a cigarette. All that Kevin ever wanted was love. By age thirteen, he had seen more violence and had tasted more life experiences than most adults see in a lifetime. On his thirteenth birthday, his mother forced him to take drugs and tried to pour liquor in his mouth. He eluded from his home. He ran to our school and our generous math teacher Mr. Alexander gave him shelter and later fostered him. When Kevin was fifteen, he went back to check on his mother. She has just gotten out of a relationship, was smoking like a chimney and was so high on drugs that she didn't even recognize him.

"After seeing what smoking and drinking would do to a person, Kevin got scared that even one sip could tempt him to drink more and eventually get addicted and become an alcoholic. He decided right then that he will be a teetotaler and never ever drink in his life. He has a beautiful soul that hated the intemperate and uncontrollable drinking of his mother, but never loathed his mom. His adoration for her never faded, even after all the years of mistreatment. He always says that he understands her situation where she couldn't handle the pressure of having a kid when she herself was a kid. In Kevin's view, alcohol is the evil, the blight that made his mom lose control over her life, and the reason why he lost his mother's love and only got to see her resentment towards him.

"Who would imagine a mother who physically gave birth would punish the child for something which is not even the child's fault to begin with. I always thought that the needs of a child will automatically become a biological priority for a mother. The local church congregation and some neighbors collectively sent her to rehab several times, but to no avail. The devil found her again and again, and in the battle between her sanity and alcohol, alcohol always won. Her health slowly deteriorated and became brittle; she was routinely shuttling between hospital clinics and rehabilitation centers. People like her have to encounter a near death experience to even entertain the thought of changing themselves, and that is what happened. Her liver succumbed to the years of alcohol abuse and she needed a liver transplant. There was very little hope as it is an expensive procedure with limited donor pool.

"But to her utter surprise, she quickly underwent a successful remedial surgery well before the damage could take her life. And to her disbelief, it was Kevin who was paying for her hospital bills, and also donated a part of his liver. When she found out that it was her own son, whom she mistreated with iniquity and abused from childhood, was the one who donated his liver to save her, she became a completely new person. Kevin takes care of his mom now, however, she quit consuming all those toxins. She wants to show Kevin how much she loves him, but unfortunately, she cannot get his childhood days back. When I became pregnant, we decided to name our child Kevin, so that she can see her son, in our son. But she got more than she had bargained for because there are some things in life for which we are never truly prepared. As such, her life has now become frenetic and antsy catching up with the natural exuberance of our messy twins, Kevin and Robin.

"Every time I think about of Kevin, I always wonder the courage, determination and perseverance he showed to curb his urge and not to get dragged into that swamp. If he had taken the drugs on his birthday when his mother forced them on him, I am scared to even muse how his life would be now. But he now spends his time and money to create awareness on premarital courting and diffuse the importance of using safety measures. Using his experiences, he makes short films on the emotional trauma that some kids go through and arranges counseling for parents in need. I couldn't be prouder of what my sweetheart has become. I am very lucky to have found him."

While Clarisse was divulging Kevin's rocky and ragged childhood, everyone sitting at the table had intermittent tears. Who wouldn't? I always knew Kevin was a strong person, but little did I know that his fortitude was forged from the battles he faced as a child in that unpredictable environment. There are some things we encounter in our life for which we are not responsible, and some things which we do not have in our control, like choosing our parents, but we definitely are responsible for what we want to be and Kevin is a prime example of 'You become what you want to be.' In such an adolescent age, it would have been very easy for him to get influenced by his mother. But he showed maturity and knew what was right for him. Life is a blend of good, bad and ugly experiences, and one should be able to differentiate between the good and the bad, the right and the wrong, and stay unwavering in the chosen path. The other good thing about Kevin is that he never stopped loving his mom, nor did he lose hope and trust in people.

As we were talking, I heard a male voice from my back. The voice said, "Hi y'all, how are you doing today? How do you like the food?" I quickly recognized the deep rich baritone voice. As I swiftly turned around, there he was: Fresco Ordell, my dear friend from high school whom we all fondly called "Fres". I was in awe. My body just stood still, mouth went dry, hands and legs grew numb, and my mind turned blank. The only part of my body functioning were my eyes, and I was conquered by tears. I was weeping so bad that there was an unyielding ferocious battle between tissues and tears, and tears clearly secured the victory. I rushed to the nearest restroom to wash my face, and Clarisse, Abi and Sydney followed me. As I got out of the restroom, Ethan, Kevin and Fres were waiting for me. I moved towards Fres, gave him a big hug and told him, "Fres, you are the reason I am here. And I wouldn't be this person if I didn't see your video that day." Fres hugged me back and tried consoling me. I do not remember how many times I told him "Thank you" in the five minutes he was there. Soon, we walked back to the ballroom. Though no one disturbed me, I could perceive that everyone was thinking about me.

Sydney nervously approached me to check on how I was doing. Ethan rushed towards us and reassured Sydney that I am fine, and that it is probably best if I am left alone for a while. Though they moved away from me and some soft music was playing in the background, I could still overhear them. Ethan told Sydney that I must have remembered my past seeing Fres and continued to tell her about the Alex he knew.

"The Alex you met today is a completely different person. The Alex we knew was a happy-go-lucky person with no aim. Though she was smart, she was never interested in studying. She had a photographic memory and could remember anything and everything after reading or listening only once. In high school, we once tested her memory by giving her thirty heterogeneous words to remember, and she spelled them back without missing the chronological order. She is also good in sciences and could solve complex math problems very easily. However, she never focused on her studies or bothered to pay attention to her grades. All she ever wanted was to become rich, marry a handsome wealthy guy, and have a family. She had a strong resolve, but a bad philosophy of life. She paid the utmost attention to appearances and believed easy money is worth the same as hard earned money. For me, it seemed like she was always in a fantasy dream from which she didn't want to wake up from. Nonetheless, if she commits to something, she gives her 100% effort, even if she doesn't like it.

"For the little amount of time she spent studying overall, I was surprised when she got a perfect score on her SAT. Albeit she didn't like studying, she got into Harvard and completed her degree just so she could be far away from her parents. Alex and I had completely different opinions on almost everything and always used to fight on issues. But I still liked her as she was smart, very helpful and a loyal friend. Whenever we were around Alex, we had lots of fun as she loved organizing raucous parties and carousing all night.

"A few days into college in 2014, we had a welcoming party where we all met Philip. Philip was the only son of the business tycoon Mark Alphie, the founder of Alphie industries. He was tall, handsome, and a rock star. He performed a solo on the welcoming day. We all liked his performance and his voice, but Alex just fell in love with him at the very first sight. Alex is someone whom anyone would fall in love with. They soon started dating. We then no longer had the parties we used to have with Alex as she was busy going out with Philip. She used to lie to us to go early to the class to be with Philip. Though Alex never moved in with Philip and stayed throughout the four years of college in the dorm, she spent most of her day time either in classes or with Philip. She only came to her room to sleep.

"Philip proposed to her at the end of our second year and they were engaged. She was on Cloud Nine when she showed her big stone to us. She said they were planning for a destination wedding out on a beach as soon as they finished college. We personally didn't like him for the way he treated Alex and we even tried to tell her, but she didn't listen. Eventually, Alex was also scared to talk to us as Philip didn't want her to fraternize with us at all. Every time they had a fight, he would to buy expensive stuff as a conciliatory gesture and to placate her. And Alex used to brag about the gift he bought to overlook the reason why they fought and to expunge the altercation from her memory.

"At the same time, Alex was also pushing herself away from her parents. It went to such an extreme that her parents would send their birthday gifts to me and I would give them to her as if they are from me. She also dwindled talking with her parents so much that she would go not talking with them for more than six months.

"I don't know what happened after our college. When I asked Alex yesterday as to what happened, she said that Philip and she are now estranged. But seeing her like this, it is like alchemy of human. Though everyone has the power and control to wrought themselves, I wonder what triggered Alex to transmute into what she is now."

Because of me, the mood was a bit murky during lunch. I guess to lighten everyone's mood and to ignore what happened, Abi snarled, "Yo...Fro, my food is all tangled, twisted and knotted. How am I supposed to untangle every strand and eat? It will take me forever to do that." We all looked at her dish, and it was noodles. Everyone erupted into a huge laughter.

At the lunch table, as everyone tried to forget what happened, Fres broke the big news of the day: his engagement to a beautiful girl named Kelsey. I couldn't be happier for him, for it was because of Fres that I was still alive. I couldn't help but remember how Fresco Ordell became what he is today, especially after that tragic event that rattled everyone during the last year of our high school.

FRESCO

Fresco Ordell and Mort Everett were two of my very close friends in high school. Both Fres and Mort were very punctual and never missed a day of school. Fres was only a month older than me and would turn eighteen only after high school was over, but Mort was six months older.

Mort was a tall, healthy and ambitious student. He had a reputation for being very diligent, intelligent, and studious. But he was not emotionally strong. An introvert with an aloof personality, and his head always buried in a book, lessons were his sole companions. Abi, Mort, and Malcolm Spike (MS) always competed for the top spot in the class. Of course, Abi always stood as topper of the class and Mort used to undergo panic attacks hearing that news.

Fres, on the other hand, was short and stout, but he was an extrovert and the best dresser in our class. His clothes were the acme of fashion. Though he was heavy built, he was very active and always in perpetual motion. He was a genial person who was loved by all. Everyone was enthralled with his kindness. He did well in studies and had the ambition to become a heart surgeon. I knew him so well that he could not conceal anything from me. Fres being a studious person with helping nature, the freshman students would ask for his help with their classwork and lab reports, and he never hesitated to offer help and guidance. One of the freshman students who rode the same bus with us is Diane. Diane, like Fres, had the ambition to become a doctor.

One day, when we were about to finish our eleventh grade and enter our summer break, Fres asked me to help buy a gift for a girl but took an oath of allegiance not to let anyone know. I chose a pendant, which he liked and bought it. The next day, I saw Diane wearing it on her birthday and the pendant looked more exquisite on her. That was when

Fresco

I solved the puzzle of why Fres misses the school bus on the same day Diane was also missing the bus. They both were coming to school before anyone else does, at least twice a week, to spend more time together.

Diane was not very talkative, but is very caring, affectionate and a happy girl. Finally, the day before our 2013 summer break, Fres revealed about his love for Diane to the gang, and that he is going to propose to her. We jumped with joy and muddled him with a jumble of ideas on how to propose, but he had it all planned. The days when they came early to school to surreptitiously spend time together, they have a hideout place and Fres decided to propose there. Ignoring his orders not to follow him, our gang trailed him in clandestine. Diane was already waiting for him with her headphones on, listening to some music, and was quite oblivious to his intentions. Fres was jittery but trying to act normal. He went and sat next to her, and as she offered him one of the earbuds, Fres anxiously took a promise ring from his pocket, bent on to her shoulder and whispered in her ear, "I can spend the rest of my life with you and want to grow old with you." Diane's response was ineffable for me to describe in words, but it was a "yes" from her. They kept staring into each other's eyes with smiles and tears, and after a while we left the place as the sight became very boring for us. As with most love stories, we hoped they would live happily ever after, but that was not destined for them.

It was during our last year in high school while Fres and Mort were leading their peaceful lives, a pallid monster by the name Doyle entered their lives. He was new to the town and had just joined our school. Doyle walked into the class and sat in the empty chair next to Fres and Mort. Doyle was an emaciated adolescent with a thick beard. His lips were turned black from smoking and he had big, deep, puffy eyes from all the drinking. Doyle is about six months older than Mort and was friends with people much older than him. He was an opportunist and into felonious activities, which we didn't know then.

Doyle tried to engender a rift between Fres and us. He fabricated lies and beguiled Fres. Fres, who was naive and accommodating, fell for Doyle's facade and soon they became good friends. It seemed to go normally for about a month until the monster started showing his true colors and his true behavior. Fres heard Doyle using profane language and also caught Doyle red-handed doing illicit drugs. Fres, noble at heart, but also a trusted confidant, with the fidelity he has towards his friends, condoned Doyle's actions. Unsure of what he saw as Doyle's virtues,

79

instead of breaking the friendship, he decided to continue the relationship and stay associated with Doyle with the intention of reforming him. As Fres could not see Doyle lead astray, he made Doyle swear not to do drugs anymore. But little did he know that he is no match for that devious and incorrigible Doyle.

Just as when a lethal invasive species comes into an area, some of the indigenous life forms are threatened, that is exactly what happened. Doyle being perfidious, slowly used his depravity to influence Fres. Though a wastrel and a loafer, he was shrewd and offered Fres an adventure. He brainwashed Fres into thinking that those who don't take or handle drugs are weak and craven. Doyle goaded Fres by declaring that only fools miss out on adventure and that drinking and taking drugs was somehow a virtue. Fres resisted and foiled Doyle's persuasion, but Doyle was not a man to give up easily.

In school, we were taught heavily about the adverse effects of alcohol and counseled to stay away from addictive habits that are ruinous. But Fres slowly started falling for Doyle's fallacious arguments and felt like a dud and a wimp if he didn't try. Then finally one day, as the bait had its effect, the peer pressure got him. Within few short months, Fres started experimenting with smoking and alcohol. Since Fres was underage, Doyle also created him an alias and a counterfeit identity to buy alcohol and abetted him to commit acts of turpitude. Fres quickly engrossed in an alcoholic debauch and became an intemperate drinker. We noticed an aberration in Fres's demeanor and he was no longer the person we knew. We never saw Fres doing drugs, but we sure suspected he was because his personality became volatile and exhibited bouts of intense behavior oscillations where on some days he was vivacious and energetic, and other days languid and irascible; sometimes he would talk sweet and amicable, and other times truculent and vulgar.

What kind of friends were we if we didn't help Fres realize that he is on the path of destruction and dissuade him? Ethan and I admonished and tried to pierce through the fog clouding his mind and feed some sense into him, but he vituperated us to leave him alone. Just as trying to shake hands with someone showing a clenched fist is impossible, our words simply thumped his deaf ears. The friend I knew very well for over five years had become a complete stranger and inimical at times. He went from gregarious to cantankerous and unsociable. He didn't care about his friends anymore and stopped hanging out with us. Blind to the consequences, he got into self-destructive behavior by abusing his body and mind. Drowned in intoxication, he started to skip classes, remiss in his studies and failing in tests. He became so negligent that sometimes he was not even attending the examinations. Fres was also once caught copying during an exam and the saddest part was he didn't even care.

Fres's erratic and repugnant behavior also took a lethal toll on his love for Diane. He stopped talking to Diane, ignored, and didn't care for her. Initially, Fres was absconding to avoid any confrontation, but he soon became apathetic and indifferent. Even when Diane tried to reach Fres, Doyle, being wile and devious, would somehow intervene and hamper her from reaching him. But Diane was also not a person to relinquish easily. On occasions where she was able to come face-to-face with Fres to confront him, he would prevaricate his way out by giving lame excuses and lies that he was on his way to meet friends and had no time to talk. After several failed bids to vehemently challenge Fres, which only tested Diane's endurance, she was somehow able to accost Fres on one fine day to bring some sense with her love and affection. But it yielded nothing but revolt and impertinent reaction from him. Diane, who has been forbearing of Fres's disposition, felt defeated and hopeless, and having reached her calibrated level of tolerance with his fractious behavior, candidly asked Fres to choose between Doyle and herself.

Fres, without acknowledging the question, walked past her wordlessly, and Diane, pained to the core, got her answer.

Doyle also made a friendship with innocent Mort, who was very quiet and taciturn. Because of his reclusive demeanor, we didn't know much about his personal life. He never expressed his feelings with anyone and also refrained from sharing his knowledge and emotions as he didn't trust anyone anymore. He would simply not respond when someone asked him a question. We all thought he was a timid guy, but we didn't know he was fighting a battle within himself. We didn't know he had an inferiority complex and low self-esteem. He thought coming second in the class was as bad as failing and the end of the world. In his opinion, there were only two grades - you get either an A+ or an F.

Mort's parents also pushed him so much into pressure to make only excellent grades, excel at sports and fine arts, and always compared him negatively to his older sister who was studying medicine. It made him think he was not good at anything. Little by little, day after day, slowly but gradually, he was dying inside thinking that he could never achieve his dreams. He developed limiting beliefs of his own capabilities and skills which culminated in abasing his self-confidence as his negative thoughts took over. Mort focused so much on the negatives that it not only weakened him emotionally, but physically too. He failed to realize that nobody is perfect, and life is rife with hurdles and negative results. He shut his mind off to out-of-box thinking and predicted the worst outcomes for everything in his life. He labeled himself an idiot, moron, and a failure.

On Mort's 18th birthday in March 2014, I called him that morning to wish him a happy birthday. To my dismay, I heard the shocking and dreadful news that Mort wasn't there in the flesh anymore. He committed suicide on his eighteenth birthday. We knew that his self-confidence was getting low, and was feeling like a loser and worthless even after trying his best. We also knew he was befuddled about his future, but in all his intricate intelligence, we never thought Mort would see the only alternate is death. We all thought that he could no longer handle and fight the pressure of all the built-up emotions, and thus finally came to the conclusion that nobody cares if he lived or died and decided to end his life. I did not understand how killing oneself was an answer to anything.

Little did we know that the reason for his suicide was much more frightening than what we thought. Mort's parents received the autopsy reports which revealed that he was sexually assaulted. His death was investigated by police and found that Mort was sexually abused in one of the school's restroom. After reviewing the video footage, it came as a shock to all of us, and especially to Fres, to know that Doyle was the culprit who assaulted Mort. Though Doyle gave authorities specious excuses regarding his presence, the evidence was overwhelming. We didn't know what Doyle had on Mort, or how he was able to subjugate Mort, or why Mort was submissive to Doyle, but I thought it is Mort's inferiority complex that made him vulnerable to Doyle.

Doyle, who was already under investigation for some larceny and embezzlement cases, was arrested, indicted, and tried as an adult in the court for drug trafficking in school premises and for sexual assault. I never saw him again, but I heard he wasn't the least bit penitent for his crimes before the judge and was later beaten to death in jail by a rival gang.

At the same time, police also searched all the lockers in our high school and found drugs in Fres's locker. Just as the rest of us, Diane also couldn't believe, though we all suspected he was into something noxious to his health and detrimental to his future. Fres was arrested for drug possession and was later rusticated and suspended from the high school for his transgressions. All we could do was only empathize with his situation. Diane felt betrayed, but she is more refined and matured than I thought of her. When I asked Diane if she could love Fres again, she said, "Fresco is my first love and I will always remember the good times we spent. But I don't think I can ever love him again. Do not get me wrong; it is not because he is into drugs. Love is supposed to be an elixir for all evil, but my love is not adequate enough to be a panacea for his addiction. My love clearly is not strong enough to pull him out of the depths of the toxic influence of alcohol and drugs. All I can do now is just wish him well and hope he quickly becomes the person he truly can be."

I had not seen Fres again in person since then. Rather than resisting arrest, he capitulated to the authorities. For flouting and contravening school's policies, and to inhibit any further proliferation of drugs, he was expelled from school. In fear that he may distribute the poison to other students, he was also prohibited to be anywhere near schools, and as a result, Fres never finished high school. That debacle brought a catastrophic collapse in his career plans and shattered his dreams of becoming a doctor.

I never went back home during my four years of college in Harvard as I wanted to be as far away as possible from my parents, but Ethan often visited Chicago during our college days and I would vicariously experience Fres's struggles through Ethan's updates about him.

I had no idea if Fres refuted the charges levied against him or not, but in proscribing him from going anywhere close to schools, I thought the judge was severe, even merciless, in his punitive actions against him. Because of the overwhelming evidence, the judge did not exonerate and exculpate Fres, but the judge was strikingly lenient to not sentence him to any jail term and instead sent him directly to rehabilitate. Chicago, like many other cities, was in financial turmoil and reeling with dearth of funds, but Fres was one of the lucky few to be chosen for rehabilitation. While he was held in the rehabilitation center, Fres's parents never paid him a visit. His parents disowned him as he brought infamy to their name and prestige. They thought he would be a bad influence on his younger siblings and would negatively impact their pride. Fres became a pariah as his family abandoned him as if he was never born.

My initial reaction was - how could a parent throw a child out especially when they are doing well for themselves? While biology makes a woman a mother, and a man, a father, it is empathy and compassion that makes them mom and dad. It is just like the distinction between a house and a home. A house is just seasoned dead wood and fire hardened brick, whereas a home is a living entity where a family loves, laughs, and cries through thick and thin. But then it occurred to me that alienating Fres was probably needed for the productive future of his siblings. Clearly, I could not judge the decision of his parents as I was not a parent myself then.

Fres certainly did pay the price for embracing destructive paths and adopting poor decisions. He lost all the wealth that an eighteen-year-old needs - he lost his friends and became strongly disliked and an anathema to everyone. His education was flung into the garbage, his career goals came to screeching halt, he was abjured by his love and disavowed by his family. It became clear during his stay in rehab that his parents had deserted him, the only hope he had at that point, thus plunging him into abject poverty.

Fres had no money and was also lacking some of the basic necessities of life. Brought up delicately in the lap of luxury and with everything served on a silver platter, he never knew what privation was. He kept blaming himself, Doyle, and everyone else for ruining his life. Though he initially wanted to run as far as away from Chicago, something inside him told him to stay. While at rehabilitation center he experienced a deep change in his thinking, became self-confident and self-aware, found his inner peace, and realized that he had the power to choose his response to his situation. Instead of accepting his situation as if someone has placed a malediction upon him, he decided to take it as a challenge.

The indigent Fres started looking for hourly wage jobs, but without any credentials or even a high school diploma, no one hired him, especially in light of his past record as he was never vindicated from the drug charges. Battered by rejections everywhere he inquired and weary to his bones, his life took a mysterious turn one day while he stopped to repose outside a motel. He was offered a job as a janitor.

Fres immediately started working as a janitor in the motel cleaning the rooms and the restaurant. And since he was the person customers saw most, they used to tell him their problems with the A/C units, or something missing in their parties or events. Instead of telling the customers to notify the front desk, Fres owned their problems and fixed them. He saw his job as a privilege to help and serve for the welfare of the customers, and not just picking out the trash. He always overdelivered on what was expected from him and those extra efforts paid off well. Two years into working as a janitor, the motel owner saw Fres going out of the way to help a customer one day and asked him what he was doing. Fres told the owner that he is doing what he was hired to do: provide customers an uncompromising service, satisfaction, and comfort. Fres's integrity and commitment to exceed expectations by doing more than what he was asked and paid to do had captivated the owner. For his assiduity, the owner quickly promoted Fres to a shift manager, delegated more work, and gained his trust.

Unspoiled by all the adulation and precipitous growth, Fres decided it was imperative for him to be austere and parsimonious to save money, and espoused abnegation of comforts and luxuries. He also diligently learned what it takes to run a restaurant from top to bottom.

I was in my fourth and final year of college, and about to start my final semester in January 2018. Ethan came back from Chicago after his Christmas break and told me another exciting news about Fres. I was both startled and exultant at the same time to hear the dauntless thing Fres did, and I hoped one day I would be able to think and execute that way. A month before, in December 2017, the motel owner summoned all his employees and asked if anyone would be interested in buying the motel. It was an unexpected and unforeseen jolt to every employee. They didn't have millions of dollars to buy the motel, nor did no one want to take millions of dollars in loan to finance the business and risk their lives. Fear gripped every one of them and sent them into a void. Disappointed, the owner went back to his office. Fres then went to the owner and inquired the very reason he intends to sell the motel. The owner told him that in the past, his wife supported and sacrificed her dreams so that his dreams would come true. But the owner's wife got her dream job in San Francisco and he wanted to support her and move to California. The owner also told Fres that he had enough money to start over in a new place, but he did not want the burden of managing the motel from a distance. He was worried that any buyer would undercut the asking price because it is his necessity to sell, and was sickened by the possibility that many of the employees may lose their jobs.

Fres jumped on the opportunity and said he would buy the motel if he can pay the owner in installments over fifteen years for a nominal interest rate. The owner quickly accepted the deal and they made an accord. Though Fres was only a shift manager, the owner had no qualms about Fres's probity, or in his ability or competence to run a motel. The owner knew very well his employee's commitment to customer service and completely trusted that Fres would excel in running the motel productively. It was a win-win solution. The owner did not compromise and was able to sell and get the money he wanted for the motel, and Fres became an owner and found his purpose in life.

Within three short years, by the time I was in the final semester at Harvard, Fres went from a pauper to the owner of a motel. He worked industriously to improve and expand the hotel business, and subsequently over the years has accreted by establishing and franchising new hotels in several cities in the US with cleanliness and guest satisfaction as the highest priority. The capacious hotel with generous staff where the reunion was scheduled is one of Fres's hotel. Audi, Abi, and Clarisse definitely chose the best hotel in the town: The Fro.

With assiduous work, Fres became an affluent person, not just in wealth, but in deeds as well. In addition to treating his staff well with profit-sharing program, he donates half his profits to impecunious families and rehabilitation centers to help mitigate pain and conducts video podcasts to encourage aggrieved people to live a clean and healthy life. His messages are poignant, causing listeners to think, regret and repent their decisions. He also actively helps them find ways to start fresh, just as his name indicates: Fresco Ordell, meaning a fresh beginning. An apt name indeed.

As I was thinking about how Fres came out of adverse situation with flying colors, I noticed him putting his engagement ring on Kelsey. I was ecstatic for both of them.

Back in high school, when the entire school was shaken by immeasurable shockwaves of sexual assault, suicide, and drugs, I was personally moved by an unfathomable depth of emotions as I wallowed in grief. I was angry, anguished, and ashamed that I couldn't save my friends. I wished I had a time machine to go back in time and warn my friends of the monster. I still cannot stop thinking how it would have been if that monster didn't enter their lives. But at the same time, no one had predicted that it would take such an enormous toll on their lives in this way.

On the other hand, Fres was an intelligent student. I was surprised to see how he couldn't control and restrain himself from the clutches of drug obsession. I also asked myself how someone could be that naive and gullible to be so easily duped. We all learned that smoking, alcohol, and drugs were obsessive, have deleterious effects on health, and are by no means a prestige to the user. How did Fres become a slave to his addictions and where was his willpower to control himself? How could a bright and active student get into the dark and dreary world of drugs and booze? How could anyone be lost and completely blinded to the fact there was a demon inside Doyle? How could Fres not see the true colors of Doyle? Fres was only seventeen years old when Doyle entered his life. Was it his age that naturally made him blind?

I always thought I was strong and resolute. But I was completely ignorant at that time that I was going to be obscured by greed, get blinded by lust for easy wealth, and was about to fall for a phony facade and drive myself to ending my life. I failed to discern the true colors of Philip, whom I thought was the love of my life. Blinded by riches, I became deeply immersed in my own false world that also eclipsed my visceral feelings and intuition. I should have known better as I was almost 22 years when I took the wrong step and married Philip. But I guess, arrogance, ignorance and addiction come in all different ages. Or, is it because when we love someone, as if it is a primeval instinct, our critical thinking in the brain shuts down and we try not to see or acknowledge their flaws? It could be that we believe we can impact and change someone by surrendering ourselves or building trust, but the brutal truth is that we don't realize we are the ones changing.

As there was a lot of talking and music in the ballroom, I stepped out and found a secluded corner to check up on my parents and children. After my call, I saw Fres walking towards me. I wished him all the happiness and hoped he wouldn't ask about what happened. He came and sat next to me and asked me how I was doing. I told him about my interview at **SYMBIOSIS**. He then asked what happened and why I had to watch his video. Though it was very difficult for me to talk about my past, I decided to divulge about my life although I wished he wouldn't ask. With the exception of my parents, I had not disclosed my past to anyone. But if I was to share my past in its nakedness with anyone other than my parents, it would be Fresco.

PHILIP

Fres knew me well in our high school days. I turned toward Fres, with my eyes lowered, I started to tell my Harvard story. "When my eyes and attention first riveted on Philip, I saw the man of my dreams. I was sure that cupid had hit me with a slick and nimble arrow loaded with imperceptible pheromones. As my brain quickly got rinsed by a shot of testosterone, a wave of impulse energy took over me, stroking my desire with amorous feelings I had never experienced before in my life. I was also sure that I took his breath away with my hourglass figure.

"But soon, my desire vanished before a doubt. I wondered if he was single, as I was certain he had a girlfriend. Who wouldn't grab a rich, tall, muscular, and handsome guy on sight? As I looked around for the gorgeous girl tethered to him and found no one, I thought I would give it a try and asked him directly. Usually, men are considered the hunters or chasers and women the choosers or pickers; but in my case, the roles were reversed. When Philip said he didn't have a girlfriend, I gave him my number and told him to call me if he was interested.

"A few days later when Philip called me, my heart skipped a beat. And as you know, I was a boisterous girl, always chatty, verbose and garrulous. But as the phone was ringing, I simply went mute, asking myself, 'What will I say?' In the next ten seconds, I was so adrift in a maelstrom of scattered thoughts that I almost risked the call going to voicemail. When I finally answered, Philip asked if I was interested in hanging out that evening. I said yes, hung up the phone, and, squealing and squawking like a monkey with a banana, jumped up and down in sheer delight. I must have tried on all my dresses to find the right one for the evening.

"Later that evening, Philip picked me up in his red Ferrari and took me to an expensive restaurant for dinner. Walking in, I thought of how we must look: Him a large, imposing figure and me next to him, about half his size. At the restaurant, I soon noticed that he was flirting with me and I found myself blushing to his every saccharine compliment. As his voice was also a sweet aphrodisiac, I let his coquetry continue all through dinner. But the thought that we would have to part ways afterward bummed me. I kept hoping he would call me the next day. He did, and we started dating.

"Though I was physically attending classes, really all I was doing was thinking and daydreaming about Philip. I felt the irrational need to be around him all the time. As our relationship flourished, without me ever realizing, Philip changed me. Because he didn't want to, and me, to associate with 'cheap' people, he made me stay away from my friends. More than feeling badly about dropping my close associates, I felt embarrassed that I did not know how to make good friends. I justified myself with the thought that Philip was showing me the affluent and cosmopolitan way of life as I was invariably hung up at bourgeois standards of the inferior, and others were just jealous of my new lifestyle. Though Philip disliked it, I did remain in constant touch with a few friends throughout college. However, those friends were my enemies when it came to the topic of my relationship with Philip.

"After our second year in college, Philip proposed me. I felt I was the luckiest girl in the world; I was on Cloud Nine. It was everything I ever dreamt about: money, lots and lots of it, and a handsome husband. As I slowly became increasingly blind to his pugnacious temperament, contentious personality, and other shortcomings, I saw only that Philip and I were exceptionally compatible. I thought we were highly remarkably congruent as a soluble solute that could dissolve and disappear in a solvent to coalesce into one inextricable homogeneous compound, and that nobody would be able to figure out which one of us was the solute and who was the solvent. Under such presumption, unlike the prosaic lives of some wedded couples, I expected we would have an intimate, affectionate, exciting and most gratifying marriage life, and that we would be the envy of many. I wanted my wedding to be no less than a grandiose affair and as such I chose for our destination wedding in the Caribbean. I dreamt an elaborate wedding for almost two years and planned it to the very minute detail.

"Deaf to all the warnings, we finally got married in June 2018, soon after our college graduation. All I contemplated during those two years of planning was that I could wear expensive designer clothes, buy extravagantly priced shoes and bags, and go to luxurious spas and on lavish vacations. I simply thought my life would be perfect with all the sumptuous paraphernalia and a handsome man next to me.

"My parents vehemently opposed but did not occlude me from marrying Philip. Though I desired them to be present at my wedding, I did not force them especially since they were so disapproving of my decision. I also wanted to invite my friends, but did not want to burden them with expenses. But when Philip promised that we would throw a reception at his mansion in Connecticut after we returned from our honeymoon, I decided not to invite any friends either.

"My married life was stormy from the very beginning and anything but palatable. It didn't take long to begin seeing Philip's true character and personality. I was foolish to choose him even after the fevered objections of my friends and family. Of course, I understood that it was normal for married couples to quibble and that there is no such thing as the perfect mate. Everyone has flaws. I thought I chose the one with flaws that didn't affect me, but I never saw the real Philip until after the wedding. I thought everything in my life was going to be great when I married the richest and handsomest person I could find. But life is not always what we hope it to be, at least for me. I soon realized that my happiness, my marriage, and my dream were just a nine-day wonder. Just two days into our marriage, during our honeymoon to consummate our relationship, Philip slapped me. It was the first time that anyone raised their hand on me. I couldn't comprehend how anyone could hit their spouse. My father never even raised his voice to my mother, and here I was with a man who hit me on the second day of our married life.

"I thought I was judging in haste and forgave Philip. After all, he was my Prince Charming. Despite my ardent attempts to overlook his flaws and drudged effort to make my marriage work, I continued to observe a capricious and extreme shift in Philip's behavior towards me. When we were dating, Philip waited for hours to see me. But after marriage, I waited for days and nights just to see his face. In the daytime, he was spending all his hours golfing, watching sports, or playing video games with his friends. At night, he went to bars and came home late. He stopped doing the little things that won me over. He didn't even notice that I was home.

"I confess it was his physical appearance and wealth that drove me to tie the knot with Philip, but I fell in love with him and genuinely loved him. I also wanted the marriage to work, partly because I had faith in the institution of marriage and my parents were my idols for the perfect marriage. But more than that, I wanted to prove to my parents, that my decision to marry Philip and the affluent life I was living as a result, was much better than they ever envisioned or could ever provide me.

"As a child, I thought all men would be like my father. I thought husbands would be caring, understanding, and respectful. But the longer I stayed with Philip, the more I missed my father. Philip became a constant reminder of what I didn't have.

"As a boyfriend, he seemed respectful, as though he cherished me. He gave me his credit card to use and he never bothered with checking my profligate spending. But as a husband, Philip took no time in assuming the sovereign authority. One day when I went shopping, the same card was declined, and I left the store humiliated. I tried to call Philip, but his phone was off. That night, when he came home, I told him what happened, and he nastily told me that I should be ashamed to ask him for *his* money. He irrationally spat that I was trying to seize control and pillage his fortune. As a result, he took away my car keys and usurped my freedom.

"While we were dating, at the very sight of Philip, everything else would go out of focus. Even the very thought of Philip made my heart race at seventy-five miles per hour, faster than a cheetah, and I loved that sensation. I felt the same sprint of my heart just a month into my marriage, but this time it was dread. I started fearing him more than loving him.

"I thought we were the perfect couple since we used to have so much fun in college, but I never thought my marriage life would be so miserable. He contradicted everything I said or did. When I proposed we go out to eat, he vociferously insisted that we stay in. When I proposed we go out for a movie, he contended that he had other commitments. I was not sure of the reason for his animosity towards me, or what I did or did not do to antagonize him. He turned squeamish and suspicious for every little thing I did, accused me of cheating on him, and started to abuse me emotionally and physically.

"When I reflected on my entire relationship with Philip, I realized that he never treated me as a human being with emotions. He never acknowledged that I had tender wishes of my own. As an exacting husband and as a despot, he treated me as an object of indulgence, and with his prurient desires, coerced me into unprotected sex at his will, solely to satisfy his appetite. He saw the marriage merely as having a girl to play with, as often as his carnal desires bit him. He behaved as though he was a monarch and all his imperious demands and edicts must be fulfilled, whether I liked it or not. He burned all my designer clothes and shoes. He never took me out of the house. I lost all my independence. I couldn't make any decisions or judgments. I became a prisoner in that huge Connecticut mansion, trapped in a dreadful marriage. I was powerless, disregarded, devalued, and disrespected. With his condescending attitude, he made me feel inferior to a termite.

"Greed, similar to love, makes us immune to censure and gutsy to any challenge. But while love enriches life, cupidity takes us to the unfathomable depths of evil, and if and when the veil of avarice drops, we are left in the abyss. That is exactly what happened to me and the worst part was, I excavated the chasm myself. Philip is shrewd and canny, and he tamed me to gain complete control over me and my mind. Accordingly, I became a puppet and saw only a lack of options for myself. Devoid of economical means to provide for myself and completely dependent on him, I became a hostage and stayed in the ghastly marriage.

"Over time, his appetite for physical abuse gradually escalated from slapping to twisting my arms, punching, hitting and pushing, and even choking. I didn't know if it was Philip's true identity which I failed to see, or if his identity suddenly changed after our marriage, or if he was trying to get an upper hand in the relationship. My initial reaction to his brute force was to stand up for my rights in the marriage and to reply in brute force. But that would mean debasing myself to his level. But even if I do, how would I dispel his darkness with my darkness, or drive away his madness with my madness. I knew it was a vain attempt to culture a tiger and change its innate behavior, but I still decided to try. Eschewing the path of violence and pocketing the insults, I returned love for hatred. But the more I responded in kindness and compassion, the more animalistic he became. Though the assaults were a presage of our failing relationship, I kept trying the means of love to win and appeal to his demonic heart.

"As the assault and battery continued months into the marriage, Philip, the incarnation of evil and the love of my life, revealed to me on my 22nd birthday that he never wanted to marry me. He said that I forced him into the marriage. My heart was shattered like a castle built on sand razed to the ground. Those words hurt my heart just as much as a rapier run through me would hurt my body. I was speechless, and felt as if I was suddenly transported into the vacuum of space. I fell down with tears flooding my eyes so much that I couldn't see anything clearly. I closed my eyes hard to drip my tears and by the time I could see clearly, Philip was gone from the room. What I did not know then was that the thunder on that day was a portent of an approaching storm.

"I would pretend to be asleep until Philip left the house. When I was convinced he had gone, I would wake up from my bed and start cleaning my wounds and tend to my contusions. However, I could only clean the wounds that were physically visible. What about the wounds he made to my soul? I felt that someone put a straw into my body and sucked out all my self-esteem and dignity.

"I was ashamed of my situation. I couldn't simply stay in the turmoil. I needed reprieve from the abuse. At last, I became aware that infinitely better than wealth is to be a pauper but rich in freedom and dignity. I decided to give Philip independence from the marriage. But then on one fateful day in December 2018, my life took a turn for the worse. Before I could extricate myself from the tyranny of wedlock, I skipped a month's period.

"Any woman who wants to start a family would be happy, but I was petrified. I had no courage to tell him. I knew I was pregnant because I had all the symptoms, but I also had no faith he would be elated by the news. I knew he would go psycho on me, yet I needed to tell him for the safety of my baby.

"As sleep was out of the question, I waited for Philip to come home. That night when he arrived, I mustered up some courage and having readied myself for some beatings, I apprehensively told him that he would soon be a father. The minute I told him the news, he went berserk. In an infuriated rage, he pushed me towards a wall and kept boxing, punching and kicking me everywhere on my body. He blasted me for being irresponsible and blamed me for not taking safety measures. But the truth was that he slapped me every time I proposed using protection and pierced my heart with his comments that I do not know how to keep him happy. For about fifteen minutes that night, I was prey to his wrath. He punched me in the stomach with his knee, choked and threatened to kill me with a knife.

"I slid down the wall crying and bleeding, but he only took my condition as an opportunity to get rid of me. He grabbed my hair and dragged me out of the house, tossing me ceremoniously off the compound. He later came back and threw my handbag at me before he slammed the door again. I surmised it was because he didn't want a dead body outside his house by the morning.

"It was a typical unforgiving bitter cold December weather in the Northeast. Snow was raining hard and howling winds were unrelentingly slapping my face. The storm outside was unparalleled to the storm of doubt I had in my mind regarding whether I would live or not. I was so frail and tremulous that I could barely walk. I was in intense pain, both physically and mentally. With the pittance of dollars in my purse, I managed to take a cab to get to the nearest bus station. It was very late at night, and by the grace of the implacable demon hovering on me that day, the tickets were available only to Chicago. *Chicago*, I thought. Where my parents lived.

"With a sore and aching body, and cold numbing me to the bone, I decided to buy the ticket. Adrift in my murky mind, I do not remember when and how I got into the bus, but I remember staring out of the window and peering through the fickle minded dithering weather and thinking that if my lust for riches had not blinded me, I would have seen the veracity of a life with Philip and been spared of this torture. As the fugitive Sun was playing games with amorphous clouds and snow, I kept looking at arable but barren agricultural lands and weeping throughout the journey. Though I kept wishing my situation was surreal, it was bitterly true that I was indeed threatened by whom I falsely thought as 'the love of my life'. He made me feel miserable and I lost my self-esteem. I had no courage to face my parents. How could I? I never deserved their love. All they wanted from me was to be strong, successful and independent in life. But I failed them. I failed myself. I failed everyone, miserably.

"As my strength began to wane after an excruciatingly long two days of travel, feeling wilted, wizened, and withered, I finally reached Chicago in the wee hours of the morning. Everyone got off the bus except me. Where to go? What to do? How to do? The life I thought I had meticulously crafted and brilliantly sculpted was upended and was left broken and homeless. A magnanimous person saw my situation and offered me a ride to a shelter. I was very grateful. I ate food after two days.

"It is said that the biggest change in life is death. What I went through that night in December of 2018 is no less than my extinction. I experienced the demise of my 'self'. There was also another death I experienced in that calamity: the death of my baby. As my unremitting pains were getting worse, especially the stomach pain, the shelter arranged for medical checkup. The doctor, who was shocked to see my condition, prescribed some analgesic drugs and ordered an X-ray and an ultrasound. As the results came in, I was told I had broken ribs and fractured bones in my hand and a leg. But those broken bones were trivial in comparison to the news of the death of my baby and that I could not become a mother again. The doctors could not detect the heartbeat of the baby in the ultrasound. Philip punched me so hard that fetus died and did damage to my uterus so dramatic that I had to undergo an emergency hysterectomy. It was in several months I had sound sleep under the general anesthesia.

"After the surgery, due to the severity of the injuries I sustained, the doctors questioned me. My initial silence did not placate them; they are responsible and accountable for reporting such abusive incidents. As the hospital staff notified the authorities, a domestic violence complaint was eventually filed against Philip with the Chicago Police Department.

"But it didn't matter for me. I'd lost everything of which I ever dreamt. I was devastated as I saw my life tearing into pieces that I couldn't even collect. The therapeutic drugs that the doctor prescribed to abate my agony proved efficacious in palliating my physical pains, but my heart and soul were completely shattered. The doctor said I was making progress, albeit slowly. Overwhelmed with emotional pain, I uncontrollably cried myself to sleep every night.

"I lingered for hours at the fireplace in isolation with putrid thoughts of my ephemeral marriage life haunting me. I constantly questioned every moment of it, berating myself. Fulfilling the natural law of the protean nature of the human brain, I would continuously vacillate between the conflicting thoughts 'Why has this happened to me? What did I do wrong?' to 'I deserve all of this. When did I become this person?' I kept myself secluded and holed up in a room as I was ashamed to share my misery with anyone. I lamented every day and night the way I was feeling about myself as nothing would mollify me. A few times in sheer disgust, I made futile attempts to hurt and cut myself to end my life as I didn't see any reason to be alive.

"My feeble emotional state led by my abominable thoughts snowballed and spiraled me downward into a hopeless depression. Despair and despondency became my best companions and hugged me like a baby clinging to its mother. Several days I would barely eat, and other days I would become a glutton. To avenge the misery he inflicted upon me, I also spent several days with malevolent thoughts of planning eye-for-eye justice. All my love for Philip had perished and I'd grown vindictive of him. Living a sedentary lifestyle, I spent my days wrestling and battling conflicting rationale.

"As days slipped away, weeks rolled by, and three months passed, I was still at the asylum. I was clueless as to what to do with my life. I had no interest in living. I was only thinking of how to end my life. I was not in a position to look around and see how others are feeling. Somedays I was in denial, other times I was self-pitying.

"I alienated my parents, the only family I had. I estranged my friends for giving me good advice. I thought no one would miss me if I died. I became consumed with wicked thoughts of ending my life and the ways to end it. Though a few times my pride came in the way and pulled me from the verge of committing suicide, other times, I failed to execute the suicide plans as my education didn't teach me the foolproof way to die. I learned that it is definitely not as easy and simple to commit suicide as to contemplate it. To my shame, I started to search online on the most efficient, pain free, and guaranteed way to die. In that process, I encountered your video and played it. To this day, I still get goosebumps thinking what would have happened to me if I didn't click on your video."

As I recounted my story, Fres and I both had tears in our eyes.

He asked which video I had seen. Before I could tell him, Kelsey stopped by and borrowed him for a minute. The video didn't have any new story. In fact, it is the story I was very well familiar with. The story of our friend Mort. But what was interesting was what Fres inferred from that incident and the new perspective from which I saw the same unfortunate event from high school. Both Fres's and Mort's lives were severely impacted and changed by the same person, Doyle. They both had choices. Mort was feeble minded and could not believe that life is worth living. He thought tomorrow would be worse than today. He felt insecure, and with his pessimistic thoughts saw his life as doomed to failure and chose to die. While Mort saw his situation as a death spell, conversely, Fres saw it as a test. His spirit emerged stronger from the test and Fres chose to fight. Not to be mistaken: he did not switch a failure into a success. Instead he changed himself and was born again into a completely new person, a second birth in one's natural lifetime. Through that video, Fres showed that there is no dead end in life. There is always a path whenever or wherever we stop. I realized that our minds are highly plastic and malleable, and self-confidence is the most resilient thing. I also learned that our reaction to distress and what we see as a possibility is all in our mindset, because nothing can help or heal a person with the wrong attitude, while nothing can stall or stop a person with the right attitude.

Though I was getting help at the shelter home to ameliorate my depressive symptoms, nothing came close to the mental tune-up that Fres performed on my mind to release me from such an emotional prison and make me realize that I still had the power to choose a brighter path. His rhetorical speech at the end of his video has permanently lodged in my memory which still resonates in my ears till this date in his baritone voice:

"What I am going to tell you next, you can find in any comprehensive inspirational and self-help book, but I want you to stop making wishes and take action right now, in the next five minutes, not after two weeks when you finish reading your first book.

"You are in a situation and condition in which you need to make a strenuous effort to turn your life around. I was once in a forlorn situation and I know it is an arduous endeavor. So, it will be wrong on my part if I delude you into believing that it is effortless or straightforward. The path to self-purification is an onerous task and is as steep and heavy as a rocket that requires an enormous amount of thrust to break from Earth's gravity. You need to rise above the opposing forces of your mind and heart. You need tremendous courage and a powerful force to overcome your past, and your thrust comes from your purpose and ambition in life, and the grit and determination to accomplish it. Though you can read step-by-step instructions in any self-help book, I will give you some fundamental principles to jumpstart your life. Remember, your revival depends more on yourself than on any external support. Just as you cannot hire a person to do your restroom business for you, you must pull your life up from the dungeon by yourself. No one else can do it for you, except that they can provide you the emotional support and encouragement.

"*Recovery from personal trauma is not just about enhancing and reinforcing self-esteem, but also a profound and abysmal personal transformation. But before you can transform yourself, first, you need to be self-aware. Stop blaming others for your current condition. Take complete responsibility for your past decisions and take control of your life. Truly apologize for your past actions and confess to those who deserve to hear you and has the right to receive your confession, and not to a brick wall or to a dark room.*

"*The basis of any personal transformation entails believing in yourself, creating or finding a purpose in life, and a vision to achieve it. From my experience, 'how' to live will never be an issue if you have the 'why' to live. Create goals, chop them down to manageable units, and take an action. Make a commitment to not quit or give up for any hurdles, setbacks, or humiliation. Your strength comes from your impregnable and indomitable will.*

"*Believe the goal is possible by believing in yourself. Develop an attitude and mindset that will attune you towards your goals. You may be coming from a place where you don't want to believe in yourself anymore. Your past experiences and current circumstances make you believe not to trust your judgment anymore. That is fine, and I understand that it is hard at this time especially when you are trying to turn your life around to believe in yourself. This is where if you have someone, like a friend or a family member, who believes in you can provide immense emotional support and guidance. But you don't need to look far away for that support. With their unconditional love for you, your parents have believed in you even before you started to believe in yourself. Don't be ashamed or embarrassed to ask for help. Any help will only benefit you in your struggle to build your internal strength. Every great person you know has asked for help at some point of time in their life. Find a mentor who would guide, support, and encourage your growth.*

"*People say to err is human. It is true, but animals also make mistakes. What makes us human is realizing and acknowledging a blunder was made, true repentance, and atonement for our past mistakes. Life has many problems. Don't run away from them or ignore them. Tackle them head on. Adversity indents us, but we don't need to be defined by those marks. Open up to someone dear in your life and start cleaning up your messes. Stop living in resentment, the poison that is killing you. Close your past. Your past is gone. All that matters now is what happens to you from this moment forward. Think this way - that you got a colossal opportunity to create a new life the way you want it. Start living for a bright future. Pain is past, penance is present, and felicity is future.*

"Someone exploited you because you were weak. Don't let anyone take advantage of you again. Take back control of your life by controlling your thoughts, behavior, and your environment. Sterilize your thoughts by removing the negative in you and substitute with positive attitude. You may have lost a lot of things to get to this place, but your talent is still with you. And remember, your future is not dependent on what you have lost, instead on what is still with you. Everyone is good at something. So, introspect your abilities and start working with things that you feel passionate about. Concentrate on things that bring you joy and confidence. Focus on polishing those skills to build your courage and put your skills to good use. Take the leap and start transforming your life. Concentrate on your priorities and goals.

"Try to get a job in an area in which you are talented. Even if you don't find a job in your area of expertise, find something that will take your mind off your past. Remember, there are many educated jobless people ready to do even the menial jobs for their survival, but they couldn't get those jobs. There is no shame in doing a low-status job. There is dignity in every job. And if you get a job, go the extra mile. With your drive and work ethics, show that you are willing to work hard and stand above everyone else.

"I will tell you again. It is not going to be easy but refuse to give up. It takes time, hard work and persistence. Everyone gets the same 24 hours in a day. So, use your time wisely and productively. Every minute you spend should serve one of the minor goals which eventually will serve your ultimate goal. Don't be afraid to say <u>NO</u> to that which your conscience doesn't agree with. And don't waste your time speculating about what others will think about you. Because the fact is, no one is thinking about you and analyzing you. Everyone is busy bothered with their own lives working on their goals. So, if you remain steadfast even in the face of ridicule and humiliation from goalless people, success will fall like a ripe fruit as a natural consequence.

"And if you ask me how to know if the progress is made in the right direction, I will tell you one thing: the most authentic feedback is the one you give yourself. Every night you should be able to gallantly stand before the mirror, and unflinchingly face yourself with courage to measure your

goals and say, 'I did good today. I didn't do anything I regret.' You may be able to lie to anyone, but not to the one standing before you in the mirror, because after all that is your reflection. You have a long journey ahead of you, but you will not reach there unless you take your first step right now. And don't wait for some felicitous or apt time. If you are trying to do the right thing, the day is always auspicious, and the time is always propitious."

JEMMA

Fres was back. The minute he sat back down, he asked me to continue my story. "But only if you want to," he added hastily.

I gave him a reassuring smile and started to reveal the struggles of my transformation. "After watching your persuasive and effective video, it became clear to me that wishing and hoping is simply unproductive and wasteful use of my valuable resources. Like you, I too felt that I don't have to run away and choose to die, and that I have the power to choose my response and change my life. I decided to turn my life around. That positive thinking permeated my mind and increased my confidence.

"I felt a newfound sense of hope. It fortified my subconscious belief that I am capable of achieving anything. Similar to the law of nature that 'one season is the natural consequence of the last', one must also believe, expect, and look forward to consequences and concomitant effects of one's decisions, either good or bad, as a rule of life. I realized the sobering fact that there is no one else to blame except for myself, and that everything I was going through is the consequence of my decisions and actions I made in the past. I decided to accept my situation and take full responsibility for where I am in my life. I decided to stop complaining about stuff I couldn't control and to quit making excuses.

"Fres, your last words catalyzed me to take the first step right then. Though there was no ambiguity in my conclusion that my parents are the only ones who deserve to hear and receive my confession, I was ambivalent as I had mixed feelings about reuniting with them. On one hand, I would be euphoric to see them after such a long time; on the other hand, I was afraid of the pain and agony that I would further cause them. But I felt that the risk should be taken and that I could not cleanse my past without mending that relationship. I knew sublime forgiveness was one of their admirable traits. I made up my mind to confess everything to my parents, ask for their clemency, make amends with them, and start a fresh life.

"Though I was in a shelter on the South side and my parents were all the way on the North side, both locations were easily accessible by train. I took the forty-minute train ride and walked from the train station to home in about ten minutes. My goal was to seek redemption from my parents and move on, though I had no idea of where to go, but I did not want to be an encumbrance. It was around 9PM when I reached my parents' home and I was pretty sure that they had their dinner and were watching news on TV.

"I was scared and apprehensive as to how they would react as I had not spoken to them since before I got married. With a blend of emotions going through my mind, trembling with fear but with a contrite heart, I anxiously and hesitantly pressed the doorbell and waited outside my parents' home, which for the very first time felt like an eternity. When my dad finally opened the door, relieving my heavy pounding heart, I couldn't muster myself anymore and started to sob thunderously with both happy and sad tears streaming down my cheeks.

"Without any hesitation or reluctance, my dad invited me in, hugged me and said, 'Everything will be fine.' I was still crying as my dad walked me into the family room like I was still his little princess. My mom came running towards me, to pacify me, and held me while I sobbed for what felt like hours. They both tried to allay and alleviate my anguish, but I was inconsolable.

"After I calmed down a bit, I started talking. I apologized to my parents for everything I did put them through, and I promised them that I would never hurt them again. I felt guilty that they didn't abhor me. They embraced me for who I am which made me regret the opinions I had of them. I told my parents everything from the moment I got married to the time I was about to commit suicide. I can't imagine how hard it must have felt when my parents heard me saying that I wanted to die. They just sat with me and listened to everything I had to say. I opened up to them, poured out all the feelings that I was suppressing over the years. My parents knew that there will be lurid details and obnoxious truths that I was about to tell them, but they listened empathetically with an open heart and compassion.

"Though it is innate and instinctive for parents to give out advice, they were quiet and didn't speak a word, knowing that I needed to let it all out off my chest. My parents acknowledged what I was saying and spoke very few times, only to say things like 'it must have been difficult for you' and 'we totally understand'. I was vulnerable, but they made me feel safe, valued, and loved. Their love strengthened me. Opening up to them was therapeutic. I had a false idea that who makes me laugh are the ones who love me the most. But that day I learned that I was wrong. Who loves me the most are the ones who sit beside me and console me when I cry. I wanted to leave the next morning in search of a new life, but my parents would not let me go easily.

"All throughout the conversation that night, my parents didn't talk about Philip. However, like any other parents, they could not digest the fact that their princess was tortured and tormented, and for his reprehensible behavior, the very next day, they piggybacked on the existing domestic violence complaint with the Chicago Police Department. Despite a few intimidation efforts from Philip down the road to retract the complaint, my parents stayed put and made sure a subpoena was issued for him to testify in court.

"Though I made up my mind to transform, my confidence was buffeted by the pounding waves which repeatedly pushed me back to the shore. The waves reached me in the form of my dread of imaginary derision from neighbors and acquaintance. For about a month, I lived in shame that people would ridicule and poke fun at me. Even though you said to not to, I unnecessarily and needlessly worried about what everyone would think of me. During that time, I stayed home in stolid bearing, shut off from the outside world. On a few occasions, I maintained a stoic face so that no one other than my parents could perceive and apprehend my true emotions. But those days were no waste. During that month, I completely opened up and my parents listened. As we understood each other's feelings, we broke through our emotional barriers and again built our relationship. I started to feel the love and trust that I didn't experience from my teenage years. My solicitous parents were always the ones who cared for me, encouraging me to be strong, independent, educated, and provided the growth opportunity, but it was lost in the miscommunication.

"Though it took me some time to pierce through the waves, I realized that one can ever please everyone and no one is perfect. Criticism is an inevitable part of life. No matter the positive qualities one possesses, everyone deprecates and lambastes others, and everyone is disparaged by others. Realizing and accepting this fact allowed me to overcome my unwarranted fears and concentrate on work at hand.

"It was April of 2019. I was in a crummy state, both physically and mentally. I could not excuse the senseless waste of time in which I indulged and decided to purge both my body and mind. After introspection of my abilities and skills, I concluded that my forte was in creative writing and vocabulary, but I was not agile with my verbal skills anymore. My talents were definitely rusted and atrophied from lack of use. I wasted no time. I decided to awake my dormant skills and put them to use. I was spending my daytime in the library reviewing books on creative writing and vocabulary building, attending classes and workshops, reading political news, watching videos of speeches by influential people, and studying the anthology of writings by great leaders and compendium of works by famous philosophers. Though I was expending a vast amount of time deeply immersed in re-polishing my skills, it was by no means a quick process of burnishing the corroded brain. Experiencing a painfully slow progress, I felt the glaciers moving under my feet but no significant daily improvement in my vocabulary. However, though the pace was frustrating at times, I refused to quit and kept my progress flowing at its pace because I knew even a modest but steady advancement would surely compound over time.

"I decided to follow every step you mentioned in your video, which also meant looking at myself in the mirror. During my teenage years, the mirror was my best friend. I would spend hours staring and obsessing over my looks while carrying out interminable questioning if I am attractive or not, and constantly assess where I stood among my friends on an arbitrary attractiveness and sexual competition scale to entice a mate. But I hadn't looked in a mirror for several months. The first few days were painfully hard, but soon I was able to look at myself in the mirror without flinching. 'Bad' is probably a benign word to describe how dreadfully I treated my body, in part due to my insanitary habits. In my futile attempts to end my life, I cut myself several times which annexed to the lacerations made by Philip. My skin has become a canvas of permanent scars. As no amount of emollient cream seem to soften the skin, I decided to use those ingrained and lasting blemishes to my advantage. I decided to use them as a constant reminder and motivation for my future goals, and to introspect and feed myself the positive thoughts. No wonder why you said to do it. And it is true that I couldn't

Jemma

delude myself in the mirror, because deceiving myself is a million times worse than proven a traitor before the world. To renovate my body, I renounced junk food, and made a commitment to wake up at 6AM and run at least four miles every day, rain, shine, or snow.

"I soon created a quotidian routine and I loved every minute of that life. Randomness vanished from my dictionary; I scheduled everything. I followed a strict discipline for every item on my agenda and would severely punish myself if I violated any. After my workout, I had breakfast together with Mom and Dad. Then, my dad would drop me off at the library near his workplace, and I would spend hours reading books and jotting down my opinions. Dad and I drove back together in the evening; though sometimes I would get lost in a good book and would not realize until the library was closing for the day. Once we were home, the aroma from the kitchen greeted us every day. And like during my childhood, we all sit down to have dinner together in each other's company. But this time, I was not looking at my phone anymore. I was grateful for how delicious dinner was and I thanked my mom for making all my favorite dishes. We talked about how our days went and I would talk their heads off with my opinions about a book I read. After dinner, I helped clean up, hugged them, and expressed my gratitude.

"But control over my body and mind was not enough. I needed to also sanitize my heart and soul. Though during the daytime, I was able to keep my mind occupied by engrossed in books, by nightfall, my heart still filled with malice, sought animalistic vengeance on Philip. Even if it meant I stoop to his level and engaged in violence, even if it meant I got only short-term satisfaction which still cannot bring my dead life back to radiance, rancor and craving for retaliation was consuming me. Just as its relentless throb, my heart was unsettled and ravenous for retribution. The internal storm was more than I could bear and was becoming the bane of my existence. Clearly, the emotional wounds were still raw and bare.

"As I was oscillating between fresh and rancid thoughts, to breed empathy in me and guide my inner self, my mom suggested I accompany them for some volunteer service work during the weekends. Unlike the sluggish progress of my English skills, the rewards of service were brisk and immense. I never thought service had such curative properties and I felt liberated from the shackles of internal strife. I was astonished to see so many altruistic people truly working to serve and mitigate a stranger's misery. And for the first time in my life, I directly saw and perceived the ordeal of another human and felt pity. That pathos and compassionate feeling provided a new outlook on the value of life and unruffled my mind and heart. I learned that grudges are inane and pointless, and those who hold them will never attain serenity in their life. It was also then I truly digested and accepted that what I endured is the consequence of my own decisions, stopped blaming Philip, and became free of animosity towards him. I gave up even the puny intention of retaliation as I became certain that it was a misuse of my emotions. I not only vanquished but destroyed all inclination and erased the desire for revenge from my heart so as not to leave even a bit of a trace.

"Though English language considers them synonymous words, on that day, I learned the vast difference between 'joy' and 'pleasure'. Just as volunteers bring the help to the needy and deliver hope, selfless noble service, service done for love and out of one's spirit and without expecting anything in return, absolutely brings enjoyment to the volunteer and gives instantaneous gratification. But I also quickly learned that it is no service if it is done for our own betterment. Indeed, service has no meaning if it is done for show or done without a wholehearted commitment to the prosperity of others. Undeniably, all other worldly pleasures are pale and feeble compared to the joy I felt that day. I also learned that happiness, one of the goals to which we all strive for, can also be achieved by making the lives of others happy and tranquil. As I punctually continued my weekend volunteer service with a firm conviction to never feed false or transient hope, I learned that hope is the last thing that dies in a person.

"Of course, happiness is subjective, but I mistakenly associated public esteem and wealth with happiness without realizing that those are ostensible pleasures. Much worse than that, enrolled in the school of hedonism, I always thought pleasure is the same as happiness and would berate my parents for never making me happy. As a lower-middle class family, we never took extravagant vacations. In fact, my parents have never been out of the country. But we didn't have a staid lifestyle either; they made sure that we went on two vacations every year to theme parks, national parks and monuments, beaches, museums, and more. By the end of high school, my greatest achievement was visiting all national parks and theme parks in the country. But I would tell everyone that I didn't go on vacation as I would be embarrassed to confess what seemed like cheap and inferior excursions. When wealthy classmates recounted their exorbitant holiday getaways to exotic places complete with exuberant concerts and lavish dining, I would feel sick to my stomach, condemn and revolt on my parents, chiding them for not taking me on exquisite vacations.

"I even vilified them for their charitable donations, screaming that if they hadn't been donating ten percent of their income to those miserable and pathetic charities they supported, then we would have enough money to go on exotic foreign vacations that I would actually enjoy. I am not sure from where I got the nerve, but I cannot believe I had the effrontery to scorn their generous hearts. Sure, memories can be made on those splendid trips and can give us profuse pleasure, but the satisfaction that my parents were getting by allocating a fraction of their income to philanthropic activities is immeasurable. The true and boundless happiness that they get by being of service is no comparison to the hedonistic pleasure I mistakenly thought of as happiness.

"As days went by, the ultimate test for my aplomb came in July of 2019 when I saw Philip again as a litigant in the domestic violence courthouse of Chicago's Cook County. At the start of the trial, I felt indebted to the laws that allow a victim to initiate a domestic violence case where they now reside instead of where the brutality took place. I also felt relieved that laws permitted me to remain in the safety of my parents while I recount that dreadful day in court. However, in a pompous display of his arrogance of power, with a colossal legal team composed of self-obsessed narcissists, the egotist Philip fiercely rebut my assertions. As if I have prophetic abilities, I presciently predicted the result like a clairvoyant. Keeping the spirit of travesty of justice alive, the case was declared a mistrial as it was my word against Philip's. Any evidence was labeled tenuous at best by his legal team and insufficient in substantiating the allegations. My parents were dejected hearing the verdict. But what came after the decree was the second set of iridescent fireworks in that month. While the first fireworks celebrated the independence of our country, the second was to celebrate my freedom from Philip forever. I was served with divorce papers to annul the marriage, and I signed them ecstatically.

"The day the trial ended, on our way back home from the courthouse, my mom didn't speak a word in the car. I am not sure if it was because the case was declared a mistrial or because I finally got independence from Philip, I couldn't sleep, and that night I also got an answer to a question I asked myself several times as to why my parents never spoke to me about Philip. I was walking past their room and I heard my mom sobbing - 'She is just a baby. How can an educated person do this to another human? I was confident until today that we will get justice and make him pay for what he did. But now I've lost faith. Why is this happening to our Jemma? I know she is not perfect, but she is not a bad person either. Our daughter deserves a fulfilling family life.' I felt warmed hearing my nickname. Though Jemma means gem or jewel, I never liked my parents calling me that name, and growing up, I would always correct them.

"In an attempt to console, my dad, with his trademark equanimity, responded to my mom by saying, 'I don't know why it happened. All I know is our Jemma needs us now. She needs support and that's exactly what we are going to do. We will stand by her and fight this together. We might have not won today, but we will. People like Philip pay for their sins, if not right away, then definitely in the future. They assume that having wealth gives them immunity, but no sin goes unpunished and I need you to trust me on this. All I ask you is that we should continue not talking about Philip before Jemma. You and I know very well that except for learning from our past mistakes, we cannot do anything about our past. So we need our Jemma to move on and have a life.'

"I couldn't keep my eyes dry after hearing them but I vowed to move on as my father intended. However, though my heart found its imperturbable tranquility and everything seemed to be going well, there was still something heavy on my soul. I tried some spiritual ways to heal and cleanse my soul, but they were definitely not for me. I understood that I should not stress and waste my emotions on trivial stuff, not to be disturbed and exasperated by daily petty things that I cannot change, and not to sweat the frivolous things as they would drain my energy, but detachment from fruits of my actions was making me indifferent and lackadaisical, lethargic and unserious about my goals and ambitions. Rather than give up attachment, I needed a gut-wrenching fear as a force to push myself into challenges. Because spiritual books only made me phlegmatic and helped me handle big problems with patience, I zealously looked for other ways to spiritually cleanse, without any side effects.

"As my rigid discipline soon turned into new habits, and with a circadian clock-like routine, I saw progress and a drastic change in myself. I also felt proud that I went to the library without missing a single day, every weekday for four months. But I couldn't even dare to compare myself to my dad, who was 63 years old and went to work punctually. What further intrigued me was that I couldn't believe how my dad managed to keep our family car running for two decades. It was same car that he used to drop me at middle school when I missed my school bus. One day, on our way back from the library, I asked him if he didn't need a new car, since the one he drove was obsolete.

"'New car?' he responded. 'Why do I need a new car? This car is my baby. Just because it looks broken from the outside doesn't mean I have to replace it'. He told me that he'd bought the car when I was four years old, and that I had pointed to the car in a magazine lying on the table. 'We bought this car for your fourth birthday. And you were a very picky girl. Every time we went shopping, you literally always picked the most expensive item there and you made sure you got what you wanted,' he said.

"I was taken aback. I didn't know how to react to what my dad said. I just leaned on his right shoulder and massaged it while he drove. He kissed my forehead and said, 'I love you Jemma ... I mean Alex.'

"With tears in my eyes, I told my father that I was sorry about everything, that I didn't deserve his love. 'And,' I added tearfully, 'You can call me Jemma'.

"My dad pretended he didn't hear anything I said and started singing a tune that went something like-

'Don't be sad, don't be sad, it's a happy happy day!
Don't be mad, don't be mad, it's a happy happy day!
Don't be rude, don't be rude, it's a happy happy day!
Be happy, make others happy, and soon everyone will be happy happy happy!
Be the reason for one to smile and soon everyone will be happy happy happy!'

"The song was one I wrote at six years old for my first-grade songwriting contest. I couldn't believe my dad remembered my silly song. He drove all the way home with my head on his shoulder. I felt like a little girl again, my daddy's girl. In that moment, it also felt a little lighter on my soul as if a part of the heavy boulder resting on my spirit had vaporized and induced vitality in my quest for spiritual sterilization.

"*This is it*, I thought. This is what I have been seeking in my pursuit of spiritual cleansing - the absolution from my sins. It became clear that I needed to genuinely repent and expiate for all my wrongdoings and my querulous behavior towards my parents. I hastily started to list examples of my barbaric demeanors towards my parents and I had no trouble filling two sheets of paper in an hour.

"It is weird how our brain selectively recalls only the negative things about a person. Things like how they insulted, how they discouraged us and said 'no', or how bad they made us feel, or what they did not do for us, but not the positive stuff. As a recalcitrant teenager displaying stubborn, intransigent resistance to parental authority, all I could only recall about my parents was them saying no to late-night parties or imposing strict curfew, controlling my social media and social life, tracking my real-time location, and the ways they mortified and abashed me by adding my friends to their social media. But I never reminisced about the times they taught me how to ride a bike, bought every gift I wanted for special occasions, and celebrated my birthdays with grandiosity and in unprecedented ways. Instead, I told them that the party sucked because one thing out of hundred didn't go the way I envisioned. In reality, my mom should be the one to be celebrated on my birthday for risking her life. Despite pervasive infertility and corresponding reproductive horrors, my mother's perseverance took her through immeasurable agony while cradling the valley of death to have me.

"My parents had trouble conceiving, but I was eventually born when my mom was 38 years old and my dad 40. Soon after I started my kindergarten, my grandparents started to disappear from the face of the Earth, and by the time I made fifteen revolutions around the Sun, my family had become small and simple: just my two working parents and myself. My parents lived in Chicago their entire life and were well-respected in the community. Being the only child, I got everything I ever craved, from trinkets to valuables. But I also got a surplus of what I didn't want.

"They suffocated and asphyxiated me in their surfeit of affection and love, and as a result I felt bereft of fun in a life filled with minor indignities. Both of them would chaperone every field trip at school, follow me like a hawk, and never let me go away with my friends. And when I said I would like to learn dancing, they enrolled me in the best ballet studio. I never missed a dance class and they never missed my ballet recitals. They were always in the first-row cheering and screaming with pure joy. But when I was about fourteen years old, a fellow student asked me if I live with my grandparents. I was mortified. I felt disgraced for having much older-looking parents. I felt such shame that I decided to stop taking ballet classes simply to avoid my parents accompanying me. At that age, I was still judging a book by its cover and people by their pulchritude. I was so focused on physical appearance, I balked at the truth that the real person is underneath, in one's heart and soul, and instead went through the teenage life chasing the allure of fleeting physical beauty while ignoring the eternal beauty and wealth of a family love.

"As I ran down the reasons why I despised my parents, I could not come up with any rational arguments. As a teenager, seeing everything that didn't please me through a magnifying glass and comparing myself to others, even the petty things appeared massively pathetic. In my vast stupidity, I completely justified my actions on things like old-looking parents, their choking love, being overly social with my friends, and their limited ability to take me to exotic locales. Though there was nothing I could offer as restitution to give my parents back those lost days of my deplorable behavior, I decided not a day would go by that I failed to appreciate them for what they did and were still doing for me. It took me a very long time to forgive myself for my conduct towards them.

"Then came Saturday, September 7, 2019, my 23rd birthday. I was so lost in my daily routine, that I actually forgot it was my birthday. What I thought would be a typical day had turned out to be a surprise celebration. My parents must have planned it like a covert operation as I didn't had a grain of suspicion that a party was in works. And as always, they went overboard, which I always felt as both suffocating with affection and gauche for prickly traditions. But that year, I loved every second of it and enjoyed the fact that it felt like a coronation day. It started with me waking up to the aroma of my mom's secret pancakes. As I was walking downstairs, I noticed all the decorations that my mom and dad put up overnight. Everything was homemade by my crafty and nifty mom. She had always been awfully creative, coming up with a new theme every year although she used the same colors. As a child, I was mortified as I thought my friends would tease me, but on my 23rd birthday, I felt admiration for her creativity, fascination, and most of all, her effort. Not to mention patience. She has the patience of an archaeologist searching for an artifact.

"The pancakes were followed by lovely marshmallow krispie treats for breakfast. Then my dad blindfolded me for my surprise gifts. A unique tradition in my family, I had always been given presents that match my age. Though my parents did this as a ritual from when I was a child, my most vivid recollection of this unprecedented and ceremonious convention was when I turned 13, the magical birthday on which I thought I would abruptly metamorphose into a "teen". That year, their silly yet thoughtful gifts humiliated me before my friends.

"Following that family custom, for my 23rd birthday, my parents gave me 23 gifts. Gifts included a pen, a few books, a diary, a new phone, a dress, a plant, a mug, a handbag, shoes, perfumes, bracelets, earrings, workout activity tracker, scented candles, spa coupons, and movie tickets.

"After opening all the considerate gifts, I noticed my dad retrieving a note from his pocket which I knew was to honor another tradition: compliments. My dad and mom gave me compliments every year, and on my 23rd birthday, it was special. My dad started reading from his note: 'Alex, my baby! You are the best thing that has ever happened to us. You are a wonderful gift to us. Today we celebrate you, and we wish you a wonderful and an amazing life ahead. Thank you for making us your parents. When you are around, the days slip away like hours, hours pass by like minutes, and just like the second hand in a clock never stops moving, we never stop loving you. You are our sunshine, the bright ray of happiness in our gloomy lives, and you are our fire, the energetic force that lights up our dreary lives. We know you sweetheart, and I believe it is time for you to know who you are. Don't be afraid to show it to people around you. No matter what happens, you have a family to correct you when you're wrong, cheer you up when you're sad, and embrace you as you are. We love you!'

"I didn't even realize I was crying the whole time until my mom hugged me and I saw her dress get drenched with my tears. She also had a big compliment written down, but watching me weeping, she decided to truncate and abridge her compliment: 'Alex, you're special. You have a quality that everyone should have, the ability to forgive. You're very forgiving, and I think it is time for you to forgive yourself.'

"Another distinctive family practice is a dance date with my dad where we dance to our special family song and my mom records the whole dance. Every year, my dad and I danced to the same song, a musical note to which I first ever rocked myself when I was about two years old. Also, every year, I would clamor and beg my parents to go out and eat on my birthday, but my mother always lovingly prepared a rich assortment of all my favorite dishes. I had no idea where she gets the endurance to prepare such extensive lunch and dinner menus.

"Though I received many gifts and compliments that day, the most invaluable and priceless gift I received was the gift of caring, unconditional love, and affection. There were several occasions during my teen years I wished I had a different family, or I had the option to choose my family. But parents and family are one's gift from nature. They are the ones who are the utmost understanding and warm-hearted. I also realized that family is bound by a subtle, invisible, and intangible yet powerful and unbeatable force called 'love'. Our ability to give and receive love defines who we are. And the very moment we lose that ability, we become a living embodiment of a barbarian.

"That birthday was the first I really appreciated everything my parents always did to make me feel special. After the food and the gifts and the compliments and dancing, I felt dizzy with joy. But my mom, smiling, told me to count my gifts. I obliged, laughing at what they could have up their sleeve. I counted and found there were only 22 items. I looked up towards my parents and they were holding the last gift, an envelope.

"You see, even with all the love showered on me, I still felt a void in my life. Up until nine months before, with a hard punch in my gut, my biology reminded me every month that I am female. But like every other woman, I did abide the difficulty, knowing a sweet blessing disguised in that pain. Though I was not fecund anymore and eternally deprived of that monthly notice of the power of incubating new life, the yearning didn't oust from my 'self' as it was invariably engraved into my brain's anatomy. If I hadn't lost my baby, I would be a mother by my 23rd birthday. Every time I saw my parents pamper me with their love, I remembered how I was robbed of my chance at motherhood and felt miserable that I couldn't have a child whom I could raise and teach him or her everything my parents wanted me to learn, and also show them how wonderful their grandparents are. I was robbed of the opportunity to understand the selfless service of what parents do to take care of their children. I wished I could go through what my parents went through with my shenanigans. But my fate was punishing me by bereaving me. And occasionally, I got lost in my thoughts of an alternate future in which I have the baby. I used to get nightmares where I heard sounds of children and on some nights, I hear a girl questioning what I had done to her. As a result, I started meditating after my four-mile run, and soon was able to control my desultory thoughts of my past and focus on my present for a better future.

"I opened my twenty-third gift to find a surprise I would never have expected: It was an application form to initiate the adoption process. I studied it quietly, smiled a thank you to my parents, put it away, but hesitantly signed it though. I didn't think adoption was for me, but I was grateful to them for their support.

"2019 became the best year of my life. I renewed myself like the Phoenix rising from the ashes. I became a student of my parents, learning civility, humility, and integrity. I sometimes thought of my dad as guileless in his simple trust of everyone, and then other times I saw him as a man of endless wisdom. But every time I thought my dad made a naive decision, I learned more about his veracity and character, which made me realize that he is a paragon of virtue. There were many such instances, but two occasions made a profound impact on me.

"One evening my dad and I stopped by the grocery store before heading home. There was a grown woman outside the store begging for money. The penurious vagabond was leaning against a wall, sitting comfortably with a baby stroller on her side, holding what appeared to be a baby, but it was completely covered up. It was one of those hot days where there was no reason for a baby to be completely covered up so much that no one could see either the legs or the face. I quickly realized the whole setup was a sham. So I decided to stick around outside the store and told my dad to get the shopping done. As usual, my mom was on the phone reminding him what to buy as he always ends up buying more than needed because he forgets the list. I waited outside for about twenty minutes with no sign of a real baby, though the panhandler was occasionally checking up on the bundle and fondling it for show. Soon, my dad came out of the store. I knew if he saw the beggar he would empty his wallet. So, I tried to distract and divert him in the direction of the car. But it ended as a vain effort. My dad saw the woman, walked straight over to her and emptied his wallet with a smile.

"As soon as we entered the car, I exploded on him, yelling how the woman was a fraud and the baby was phony. In his quintessential comforting tone, my dad replied, 'I understand my dear. I am almost quite sure it is bogus. But, what if-- just think about it for a minute-- what if there is a very slight chance that there is a baby in there. I would feel guilty for having the ability to help her, but did not, because I assumed something. And if I assumed wrong, I would never be able to salve my conscience. I will not be able to go to sleep tonight with that guilt on my chest. But now, I relieved my conscience. I am willing to be deceived a hundred times, but I cannot live with the anguish and remorse of 'what if?' And if the lady is really trying to raise a baby, what I gave her is in fact scantily enough.'

"With that lesson, I learned that if we are in a position to help someone, and in most cases we are, we should. I have seen people who gave money to gain notoriety or because they expect more in return for their gift. But when my dad gives money, he doesn't do it for either of those reasons. Though it may appear as a selfish act of absolving his conscience, he gives joyfully.

"My second lesson was on one of the weekends we volunteered at the soup kitchen. Just as we pulled up to our driveway, we heard a metallic bang from behind us. When we turned, we saw a medium-sized delivery truck inadvertently hit our mailbox, while reversing, after making a delivery at our neighbor's. I quickly ran into the street, shouting to get the attention of the driver. Two large men disembarked from the truck, telling me they were going to stop anyway. I didn't trust their words as it appeared to me they were trying to abscond. We all inspected the damage: The cantilever metal bracket bridging the mailbox to the wooden post had been detached and twisted beyond repair. The two men asked what we should do, and my father simply told them that all he wanted was a working mailbox. To that, the men said that they would bring a new bracket from the hardware store and will fix it. My father agreed, and the men left. I couldn't believe my father's naivete in letting them go, but I remained silent.

"Over the previous two decades, we changed several posts and mailboxes from basic two-piece wooden post to durable polymer based decorative posts after someone accidentally hit it and fled without leaving a note or taking liability. If history had anything to teach my family, it was that it was time for us to pay again for someone else's mistake. But to my amazement, the men were back in forty minutes with a bracket and some tools. I didn't think they would come back. It was their chance to flee. But unfortunately, the metal bracket they bought did not fit into the holes of the mailbox frame. My father even supplied additional tools to make it work, but it proved an unproductive and fruitless attempt. After vainly trying for over a half-hour, we concluded that we must buy the bracket by the same manufacturer to match the holes for the screws. The two men again offered to return to the hardware store to buy the correct bracket. My father acceded and let them go again. This second time, I was certain they would not be back. But thirty minutes after they left, they were back again. Seeing them return for the second time completely reversed my stance on their character. I felt pity for them, however, they told us that the specific bracket was not readily available in the store and must be ordered directly from the manufacturer. They asked my dad what to do next. My dad said that he would order the part and install it himself. The men gave my dad $30 for the cost of the bracket, had a good laugh about how they lost half of a day working on it, and left.

"I was a bit shocked to see my dad accept the money from those poor drivers. Though it was their fault hitting the mailbox, it was an unwitting mistake. A pure accident. Added to that, they tried their best to fix it. My dad never compelled them, and in fact was nothing but helpful and kind towards them. I did not want my dad to accept money and dishonor himself. After the truck left, I asked if accepting the money wasn't a bit disgraceful. In his quintessential reassuring tone, he replied, 'Dear Alex, I know it looks shameful and I am well aware that it was an accidental mishap. But any effort to reject money to clean my conscience will only burden theirs. They are well-principled and ethical people. I need to let them believe they fixed the damage. Otherwise, they will be stuck in a quagmire of self-judgment and moral distress and have to live with that guilt. More important than soothing our conscience is relieving others.'

"As always, I hearkened to my dad's words of wisdom and learned that the virtue of great character also comes with great responsibility of assuaging another's conscience. I also concluded that the characteristic difference between 'human being' and 'being human' is character, and that though we are all in the same human flesh, who we really are is revealed by our character. My father always said: Though the concept of human evolution has led to advancements in science and technology, actual human evolution and survival is built on the growth of character.

"Though my dad is very kind-hearted and mellow, he is no hermit or an ascetic when the security, dignity and self-respect of our family is on the line. Even at his ripe age, he still workouts regularly. My parents are not only my biggest pillars of support, but they are also my strongest defense for safety and security. Cultivating my skills and living happily enamored in the bosom of my family, the depressing memories of my married life were evaporating and becoming evanescent. Ten months passed by with the blink of an eye.

"It was early 2020s and political campaigns were in full swing for elections later that year. With my Harvard degree in Journalism, replete with knowledge of mass digital media, public relations, social media marketing, and scripting, I decided to put my education to use and get a job in one of the election campaigns. I had several ideas as to how to use technology to positively impact the campaign and make new connections with potential voters. I approached several campaign offices with my ideas, but I was already late. The campaigns were in full swing with all the campaign's operational infrastructure, media management teams, field organizers and staffers. Every position from campaign managers to secretaries and aides were assigned. I found rejection everywhere I went.

"The one place I went, the campaign office of Walter Colwart, an independent libertarian seeking to get elected for the first time to the House of Representatives in the United States Congress, told me that the only job they had available was essentially a secretarial job – which includes mundane chores such as printing press release papers and stuffing envelopes, ensuring a reservoir of office supplies are at hand, and buying lunches for staff. It wasn't what I was looking for, nor it was much of an opportunity, but it was still a job. I was taught by my parents that an infallible and foolproof test for the sign of a civilized person is the one that tests the person's understanding of the dignity of labor. Moreover, as you mentioned in your video, there are many people out in the market who do not even get the job opportunity I got.

"I wasted no time. I immediately accepted the job and started right away. My first day was dreadful. Occasionally, I had tea with an infusion of lemon or honey, but I never tasted coffee in my life and my first task on the job was to make it. The first round was so viscous that the coffee didn't even dare to exit the decanter, and the second round was the opposite, plain watery. I probably made at least five rounds that day, while sampling a cup from each round. And well, caffeine for sure is a diuretic; I can attest to that after that day. Except for a requisition I filled out for office supplies, nothing went well and I must have apologized about hundred times that day. But soon, I became an adept coffee maker and even more adroit at handling office errands. It was a small job, and though far from the position I was targeting for, I still put my heart into it. Because of the type of job, I was supposed to be the first one at the office and I made a commitment to myself to never be late. I planned and organized my days the day before for less frantic commutes and more peace of mind at work.

"I always kept my ears open for any opportunities to grow. Then one day in April 2020, a staffer who assists the campaign manager got sick and I was filled in as a surrogate for the next three days. It meant shadowing the campaign manager and Mr. Colwart. On the evening of the first of the three days, I learned that Mr. Colwart was looking for a tie that he saw in a magazine to wear for one of his television interviews, but none of the staffers were able to find. Though I was only filling in for the sick staffer, I decided to take it upon myself the task of finding the tie. What I thought would be a facile chore turned out to be an onerous undertaking. I left no store in Chicago untouched, no website unvisited, and even went through my father's tie rack. After several days of unrewarding efforts, I found a tie by a different manufacturer that was eerily similar to the one in the magazine. I impetuously bought the tie.

"I was in high spirits the next day and being the first one at the office as usual, I left the tie in Mr. Colwart's chair as a surprise gift and a note with my name on it. I was preparing in my mind how to respond when Mr. Colwart thanked me for the tie. I wondered if I should just say 'you're welcome Mr. Colwart' or 'no problem; it's my pleasure' or 'glad you liked it'. But to my utter surprise, Mr. Colwart's reptilian campaign manager took the entire credit for finding the tie and never mentioned my name. No wonder why I disliked him from the very beginning, however, in part due to his immodest nature and brusque manners. I was a neophyte in politics, but I couldn't stomach he erased my effort. I was bitterly disappointed at first, and then got a little angry thinking that this is what happens in politics, a crooked profession. I went above and beyond of what was expected from my position, but all I got in return was petulance and disrespect. It then occurred to me that it is probably a law of nature; that there are really two groups of people - ones who do the actual work, and others who take credit for it. I was in the second group before. Back in high school, I plagiarized homework from my friends, never gave them credit, and handed in the derivative assignments to the teachers as if it was my original work. I never ever thanked them for helping me out with my homework. After what the campaign manager did, I experienced firsthand the feelings that my friends felt.

"Despite the lack of recognition from the campaign manager, I decided to stay in the first group. Certainly, one can accomplish more and there is much less competition in the first group. At the end of the day, no moral person exists who would not feel happy doing the work by themselves than passing the work off as their own but accomplished by someone else. Without a doubt, iniquitous and nefarious ways of achieving success or glory carry us to our destination faster than the ethical and virtuous ways of achieving the same. But definitely in the process of achieving the end, the wicked person sacrifices their humanity and becomes a savage animal.

"Learning a new lesson everyday about human character, work politics, and political politics, I persisted in my job, and by the summer of 2020, work became busy and erratic. Some days were more chaotic and haphazard than others, but most days were imbued with negativity that is widely pervasive in the political field, and saturated with defamatory allegations and vitriolic attacks from the opponents. I became completely absorbed in my work and it became my world. But my yearning to write at least one speech for Mr. Colwart had not subsided. Though most of the time all I got was a cursory look, sometimes my job permitted me to fix errors in his speeches and press releases. However, I knew I could contribute more than just secretarial support. I kept waiting for the suitable time and the opportunity to present itself to show my potential.

"It was late August 2020, about two months prior to elections, when Mr. Colwart called an emergency all-hands meeting. Everyone working in the field office was in the conference room when Mr. Colwart delivered the appalling news. He had slowly been losing support from wealthy donors as he resisted warping his views to fit towards the donor's agendas, and it was depleting campaign funds. Not only this, but those big pockets started patronizing Mr. Colwart's primary opponent, a demagogue appealing to people's prejudices, and who with his bombastic rhetoric, political chicanery, and grand promises was willing to do anything to get re-elected. The exigent crisis meeting was convened to discuss how to stop the hemorrhage of big donors withdrawing their support.

"Assorted ideas were thrown out by several members of the caucus with the common goal of winning. The ideas seemed equivocal, but most importantly hypocritical to the character of Mr. Colwart, because the propositions called for temporary to permanent changes in his policy stances. Some members even insinuated, though careful to suggest via innuendo, that we cast aspersions and spread propaganda against our primary opponent to savagely assail and sorely damage his character.

"After a while, as the ideas started to dwindle and everyone started to mutter, I sensed that the meeting was about to conclude. But Mr. Colwart, who patiently listened to all the politically expedient proposals, was in despair. Though he was wordlessly taking notes, his disapproval with all the proposed game plans and discontent with his team who couldn't fathom his underscored commitment to his principles was obvious to me. I could sense his hesitation as I had previously proofread and amended his materials before printing, I perceived integrity in his moral beliefs. And unlike the vacuous and nebulous ideas of our unctuous opponent, he had calculated methods and policies that would work for the betterment of common people. I thought a person like him, with a high degree of moral rectitude, shouldn't forsake his ideals for mere money; after all, character and candor are more invaluable than political power.

"I couldn't let Mr. Colwart cross the moral demarcation. Though I was just an administrative assistant, I didn't care if others would think of me as presumptuous. I decided to give my two cents. I quietly stood up and said 'I am sorry to interrupt this meeting, but I feel the need to speak out. The bright people in this room are suggesting changing what Mr. Colwart truly believes in, and I know for sure this change conflicts with his ideals. We should not be worried about losing some wealthy donors' support, because their ulterior motives conflict with our principles. Instead, we should be scared that we will not be able to do good for the people. Our next step becomes clear once we decide whether we choose to stick with our principles or ditch our ideals, whether we choose to do good for the common people or advance the schemes of big pockets. I believe that the policies should not be imposed upon the people by force, but only if the majority of citizens want it. Once it becomes clear to the public that your campaign is not to yield profit to the big pockets, but purely with the intention of service, once it becomes clear to the public that your policies will help them than to punish them, the public will support you financially, though in small and moderate amounts, and even take up the responsibility to elect you, which will be a glaring testament that you have the right policies. Winning is fun and exciting. But more than the fact of *who* won, *how* the person won gets more attention. Mr. Colwart, you have pure intentions. But if your actions are adulterated, they can never justify the positive outcome. If you are interested, I have some ideas to optimize the campaign with the small budget we have, while not deviating from your ideals.'

"I was done talking and there was utter silence in the room. My eyes were so glued on Mr. Colwart that I didn't pay attention to what others were thinking of me. I could sense that he was relieved. With his usual contagious smile on his face, he said, 'That's all for now. Keep up the good work,' and adjourned the meeting. I was later summoned to his office along with our campaign manager. I spilled all my ideas, which he welcomed, and we spent hours surgically evaluating the feasibility of each overture and our ability to execute in the limited amount of time we had before the elections.

"Over the next two months, the three of us worked closely, and we implemented many ideas I proposed. I was also given the opportunity I was craving for months: I wrote a completely revamped speech, which was pitch perfect, neither grandiloquent nor understated. He used it as a template for all his addresses. As the campaign's formula was revived, poll numbers increased. I became so inordinately confident that I also worked on his victory speech. But in the short amount of time we had to rebrand ourselves, public support reached only to a level that didn't help Mr. Colwart win the elections against the incumbent congressman. The defeat was not a close call, but also not an ignominious loss, because he won a larger battle of not sacrificing his principles. For this, he secured respect.

"After the campaign dissolved in late 2020, I was back to square one, pondering my next step. By virtue of my natural inclination for news and media, I decided to start a blog called "*Alex Opinion.*" I was taught that facts come first, not first to report, so my motto for the blog was to never deviate from the strictest facts and I considered that I failed in my duty if I wrote anything that drifted from the naked truth. I also made a conviction to never exaggerate, never include extraneous details, never write an article merely to please, and never post without a serious thought. I was inundated with comments, some friendly, some bitter, some scathing. That endeavor also educated me and made me truly and thoroughly understand the responsibility of a journalist. Though it was progressing well and I became busy with managing the blog's content, comments, and correspondence, the work was far from satiating me and I still felt a sense of emptiness in my life.

"It was February of 2021 and I was completely clueless as to what to do with my life. Just then I remembered your words. My parents were watching TV, waiting to hear the triumphant news from SYMBIOSIS, and I asked them for advice. It was the first time since my teenage years that I asked them for guidance. Previously, when they offered me advice I never took it. But this time, I listened. That communication also made me understand how much I mean to them and how much anguish and grief I caused them over the years.

"All I ever wanted in my life was to marry, but marriage was what had ruined my life. My parents never asked me to marry again as they knew very well that it would take me time, a long time, to start trusting a stranger again. They also knew very well that they cannot be with me, buttress me, forever. For me to become strong, independent and self-sustaining, they suggested and encouraged me to continue my studies. But it meant I had to start all over again. As I was pondering the suggestion, I serendipitously saw Ethan on TV announcing the first ever asteroid mining.

"Seeing Ethan announcing to the world his accomplishment made me feel embarrassed about my achievements and further reinforced my resolution to augment my education. I decided to go back to school, but I didn't want to encumber my parents especially when they were close to retirement and already spent money that was supposed to go into their savings for my college education. I made it certain that I should find a job to support my studies and enroll as a part-time student that fall to earn my MBA. I was fully committed to furthering my education. I applied for a teacher position in every preschool, elementary, and middle school I could find in the area. After several rejections, I got a call from a preschool. It was looking for a full-time caretaker for an infant class. I met all the criteria and was immediately appointed.

"On my first day, as soon as I entered the room full of innocent infants, I couldn't stop my tears. It's the cutest thing one can see. Babies are little miracles. A mom then came to drop her infant and I held him so that his mom could kiss the baby goodbye. I was worried that the baby's tactile response to a new face would be crying, instead he smiled. I spent the whole day wiping, feeding, rocking, some time playing with the babies, and with the exception of one infant's post-feeding regurgitation, it was a magical day. Before I realized, the clock turned to evening and the babies started to leave. My mom came to pick me up and I couldn't stop talking about the babies. My mom told me tricks to make kids burp after feeding, which I couldn't wait to try them the next day. Soon I was looking forward to going to the school every day and meet the little angels. On weekends, I followed my mom and dad in their community volunteer service.

"It had been about a year-and-half since I reluctantly completed and signed the form in the envelope my parents gave me on my 23rd birthday. I was initially hesitant, but I finally complied, knowing their gifts were always judicious and that they knew the right things for me. The

Jemma

reason I was initially unwilling was because I wasn't sure I could love someone who was not born from me. I didn't know at that time that I didn't have to physically give birth to shower love. But my time at the preschool tending to infants taught me that I could be a mom and still spread the love even if the child is not born from my womb. That experience helped me to gain perspective that love is omnipresent and a child is the biggest blessing. I was glad that I signed the forms on my birthday. But adopting a child is no joke. It takes financial and mental stability to get through the excruciatingly long years of waiting to be bestowed the honor and title of 'parent'. Suddenly, I couldn't wait any longer and the anticipation was killing me. Every unknown call I received, I wished it was from the adoption agency.

"Finally, in May of 2022, I became a mom to my ethereal daughter, Laila. The two-week-old angel simply took my heart by storm. Though I was well-prepared for this jolt, my life quickly went into shambles trying to handle the job at preschool, my part-time MBA program, and caring for a newborn. Thankfully, I am blessed with parents who are always present to pull me out of the disarray and put me in track. Two years after I became a mom, I graduated with my MBA. There are things in the world which money cannot buy, and my convocation day is one of them. My parents exploded in unbridled joy, their eyes filled with happiness, and I wanted to freeze that moment in time. I had never seen my parents that happy, proud, and honored. I treasured that moment and hoped to rejoice those moments in my life with my child.

"Laila grew up so fast that I forgot the sleepless nights, the stench of filthy diapers, and the trials and tribulations of taking care of a newborn. Baby lust had swept me over and my heart craved again for that whimsical experience, and the tender feel and smell of a brand-new baby. And about a year ago, in October 2028, I was blessed again by the adoption agency and I became a mom to my son, Luke. I always wondered if he is born with an invisible magic wand because his smile uplifts any gloomy face. While Laila made me a mom, I adopted Luke to give him a mom.

"Though Philip was a noxious chapter in my life, the Alex you are seeing now is a practical impossibility if I didn't encounter him. In addition to my parents, I have another guiding beacon in my life. It is you, Fres. I thought it was by luck I came across your video back in the shelter; my parents thought it was by divine grace. Nevertheless, I kept watching your other videos. Unbeknownst to you, my idolatrous honor and faith towards you made you my virtual mentor. Fres, your videos became a spiritual encyclopedia that I would refer to in challenging situations."

After hearing my story, Fres looked at me and said in a serious tone, "So, Jemma is your nickname and you never told us while we were in high school. Yo girl, you robbed us the opportunity to tease you." We both had a good laugh, realized that we had been away for a while, and decided to rejoin the reunion.

As Fres walked me to the ballroom, he told me to give him a call whenever I need help and that he now understood why I did not attend the previous reunions. Indeed, though I received the invitations, I had justifiable reasons for not attending the earlier two reunions. Although our 5-year reunion was in Chicago, I was not emotionally stable as I was going through domestic violence trial in July 2019; and as for the 10-year reunion in Hawaii, I could not afford financially as I had graduated with my MBA just a month before.

CLARISSE

When I returned to the ballroom, the men and the women had formed separate groups and were discussing something. As I glanced the groups, I saw Clarisse at one of the tables and quickly joined that group. It appeared everyone was discussing their love tales and wedding stories. There seemed to be a tacit understanding that I wouldn't be asked any questions about my relationship status. However, I would get to listen everyone else's story. But to my bad luck, everyone had already disclosed their story, including Clarisse, and only Abigail was left.

I was intrigued. A person whom I never thought would fall in love because of her hectic schedule, fell in love and got married. How? I wondered. Though Abi tried to escape from revealing her love story, claiming that it was boring, everyone vehemently insisted. How could the love story of a pop star be drab? When Abi finally caved in to our unyielding pleas, she was blushing as if it is her first time recounting it.

"I guarantee that you will get bored with my story," she said, folding her hands on the table nervously. "It's not hot; it's actually not even a love story. I saw Adam for the first time during the welcoming party at MIT where he gave a mesmerizing performance with his band. Because of my interest in music and art, without consciously realizing, I felt a natural affinity towards him and we began spending a lot of time together. When he created and played music with his dexterous fingers, compressing gently, yet swiftly moving along the keyboard or when plucking the strings of the guitar, I wished I could do a functional MRI scan of his brain to map his neural networks to find the source of his deeply seductive and expressive music. We always talked about music and nothing else. As I never cared to ask, it was not until four years later that I found out that he was in fact a law student, and that music is his passion.

"I was done with my Master's and starting my Ph.D. when Adam got his major breakthrough in his music career. Though he studied law, music was always his first priority. He received a contract with a production house which was also ready to sponsor his countrywide tours. It was then he came to me while I was in the pathology lab. He informed me of the opportunity and later proposed to me by singing a ballad and finishing it with, 'Will you be the microbiome of my life, forever?' I wasn't expecting it. I stood there, calcified, wondering if it was the right time to decide about my future. I didn't say yes right then because I wanted to tell my family first. But when I called my parents and sisters, evidently Adam already got an okay from everyone in my family. Just before he was about to leave for Nashville, I told him yes. However, it was a very important epoch in our individual lives. We both knew that we shouldn't be making rash decisions and that focusing on our careers was the right thing to do. For the next couple of years, I was busy with my Ph.D., and he was busy composing albums in Nashville. We decided to get married only after my Ph.D. And lucky for me, I don't have to separately remember the date we first met, because it also happens to be the date we first got married. Yes, I married Adam twice within one month, first in India and then in the US. My parents were the event managers for the India wedding and Adam's mothers handled the wedding here."

* * *

It was about 7PM on Saturday, December 15, 2029. Dinner was announced along with the list of people who couldn't join the reunion. When the reader got to the last names beginning with "s", everyone at our table grew angry hearing Malcolm Spike's name. According to the table's consensus, it was a mystery whether or not he had even been invited.

Malcolm was many things, but moral was not one of them. He used to go by MS because of his initials. But by the final year of high school, he got several monikers and MS meant something else. Some said it meant Mad Scientist, some who recited the dictionary like a religious text said it meant Mendacious Student, and some others, Moral Slayer. He earned those sobriquets with his flawed personality and conduct.

When I first entered high school, the reputation around the school was that Abi and MS are a match to each other in intelligence. But while Abi had an attractive nature, MS had an odious personality. He was repulsive in part due to his obsessive-compulsive disorder and rampant germaphobia. Understandably, he didn't like anyone touching or moving his stuff. And since teenagers like to do things that make others mad, we would move his papers, change the location of his book, or hide his pen, and would throw in an innocent gesture when he became all red and panicked. He would not play outdoors as he was afraid he would soil his shoes and clothes. MS was so overly fastidious and extremely obsessive about cleanliness that he would call in sick the next day if someone sneezed near him. His entire manner was just repulsive.

But his quirky idiosyncrasies were nothing compared to his character. We all saw MS's true colors during our eleventh-grade science fair project. The theme of the competition that year was MARS. A maximum of two students per team need to create projects to innovate and develop technologies to explore and prepare the desolate landscape of the Red Planet to be our next paradise. The results were not surprising as we were accustomed to Abigail winning every year. Abi questioned if Cyanobacteria, through the process of photosynthesis, could produce oxygen that resulted in the 'great oxygenation event' and create a breathable atmosphere on Earth some billions of years ago, why not use that same bacteria to make a steady supply of oxygen on MARS and trigger an ecological transformation? She constructed a small scale biodome and created some of the harsh conditions of the red plant. Using one species of Cyanobacteria, she showed that the bacteria could thrive and produce oxygen even in the bleak low-light conditions. Naturally, she won first prize. Audi and Ethan did a project together; no one knew what it was, because it spectacularly exploded before they could turn it in for review and were consequently excluded from the competition.

Mort and MS formed a team. It was no secret. Every student knew they were a team as everyone saw the two working together and even thought that those two smarts combined can nudge Abi from winning the fair. Merging their extensive expertise in eluding people, consolidating their obsession with avoiding irritable circumstances, and using an autonomous rover built by someone in the previous year, they decided to program it for obstacle and hazard avoidance on MARS's rugged terrain. Though MS is sharp and brilliant, Mort did most of the coding.

When the project was finally submitted, knowing Mort's weakness, MS astutely decided to drop Mort's name and only listed his name. Mort being an introvert, did not utter a word to MS's deceit and dishonesty. MS won the solo second prize.

We all got suspicious. After the fair concluded, we interrogated Mort. Mort divulged that he was the one who wrote the rover programs and could even prove it. When Mort wrote the code, for easy retrieval, he tagged each section of his code with unique identifiers, a set of numbers and codes which have a meaning in his life like his or his sister's birthday, his favorite books and who gave them to him, etc. As the coding was done in some arcane computer language, we called in Audi as an arbiter. When she checked the opaque code, it became evident who wrote it, and MS couldn't justify what those identifiers stood for. Despite overwhelming evidence, the arbitration failed as MS, with his untenable explanations, adamantly insisted that *he* was the one who wrote the code, contemptuously refuted the findings, and decreed that he deserved full credit for the project. MS wanted to win, but it didn't matter how he achieved that win. All he cared about was being at the top of the pecking order in the student hierarchy. After that bitter incidence of MS's perfidy, Mort felt betrayed and stopped trusting others. It also became clear as daylight for all of us that MS's character was marked by duplicity and insincerity. As a result, no sane person wanted to be his friend. He for sure was adroit in his deceptive tactics and adept at repelling people. Accordingly, we branded MS manipulative and mendacious, hence his nickname.

When someone at the table asked if anyone knew what MS was up to, Clarisse hesitantly muttered that she knew. She unwillingly admitted to knowing where MS currently was, as if it was a stigma or a crime to know. Clarisse helps businesses market their products using digital advertising, and in that process, she had met MS a few years ago. From what she said, it appeared that MS collaborates with real estate tycoons who sponsor his research team to adapt the quality of desert sand. He had written a few books and is also a guest lecturer at Yale. Apparently, as part of his research project, he had worked in the arid climate of the Middle East for few years to analyze the sand and process it to lower its salt content and clear the impurities to a quality level usable for construction. Everyone at the table exploded into wicked laughter visualizing MS standing outdoors in the bone-dry temperature to study sand quality. Fittingly, he was still a germaphobe. Clarisse knew this because when his elder sister had a baby few years ago, MS didn't even touch the baby. According to him, babies are covered in germs and are carriers of disease.

Clarisse also got to talk with some of MS's disgruntled and indignant staff, and they poured out their grievances about how short-tempered and treacherous he was. To fulfill one of the epithets he earned in high school, Mad Scientist, he would go maniacal on his staff and would insanely waver between asking to provide redundant and detailed notes in the emails, and then saying that he doesn't have enough time to go through the elaborate long emails and that emails should be short. He also earned the reputation for not giving enough time to review the files or results and demands answers quickly and at odd times. Clarisse, one of the organizers of the reunion, cordially invited MS, but the haughty MS in his typical aloof manner and with all his undue smugness declined the invitation with an impertinent response.

It was always pleasant to meet good old friends and Clarisse Jash belongs to that group. She has become a prolific public speaker and was adroit at influencing through social media. One may like her or dislike her, but none can ignore her. Such is her charisma. People just want to hear her talk, because when she talks, it's so soothing that one feels like they are listening to a melodious song.

Clarisse owns a production house with skilled writers and flexible staff with profuse skills pliable to handle manifold areas of interest from performing sketches to creating content on social media like educational videos, blogs on science and technology, cooking and photography, fashion, interior decoration, and other nifty tricks. She doesn't just adumbrate the content. Instead, with alacrity, Clarisse exhaustively researches on the latest trends in each field and then produces web series on those topics. In addition to creating social media content, Clarisse also educates, motivates and helps businesses to be the bellwether in implementing latest emerging technologies and trends, and to market their products using digital advertising.

All through the high school, Clarisse had stage fright and couldn't get on the stage to perform or speak. I vividly remember the tenth-grade language arts English writing class in which Clarisse wrote a beautiful speech but couldn't face the stage due to speech anxiety. She initially received an F. Growing up, Clarisse was always scared of what others would think of her. She would worry about the judgment of others and always feared people might not like what she suggested. Thus, she suppressed her opinions in fear of rejection.

It felt implausible that such a person has overcome her fear of public speaking and has become an eloquent speaker and hosted various shows educating youth with pragmatic ideas and empirical approaches. Curious to know, I asked Clarisse what sparked the phenomenal change and set her off to allay her fears, and to eventually become an influencer in the digital arena.

Clarisse said in a poised tone, "By the end of high school, several small things had impacted me emotionally and their cumulative cascading effect triggered me to change, but the real transformation happened during college. In fact, no offense, but you were also one of them who contributed to the torrent of emotional insults that provoked the change. I always had crush on Kevin; however, I was timid and never could directly express how I felt. I had some failed endeavors in conveying my feelings to him, and Tanya, under the guise of helping me, tricked and belied me. I was upset and cursing myself.

"Few months before the prom, when the prom committee was formed, I wasn't sure why Abigail selected me, but I was happy that Kevin was also in the planning team. I felt that hope was still alive that I could confess my love before school was finally over and I left Chicago for Georgia Tech. I went along with the prom committee to select and finalize the venue, decorations, food, DJ, songs, entertainment, invitations, tickets, and for fundraising. It was probably Abigail's way to help with my glossophobia. I thought moving more closely to Kevin would help me overcome my anxiety, but I never leapt over my courage threshold to speak to him.

"About two months before prom, everything from budget to venue was set. Abigail and I were tasked to write the ceremony script. Around that time, it struck me that it would be the last few weeks that I get to spend with Kevin. I couldn't accept the feeling of not seeing him again. I mustered up some courage and planned to ask him to be my prom date and to have a dance with him. As I was writing the ceremony script and shredding several drafts in the process, I was also simultaneously working on how to ask Kevin to prom and inquire if he likes me.

"I still remember the day. It was the last Monday of March 2014. I was preparing all weekend how to pose the question and decided that the only way to do it was by asking through text message. As I typed the message on my phone with paucity of confidence and an abundance of uncertainty meandering through my brain, before I could hit send, you, Alex, came to me and said, 'Done'. And when I asked you what was done, you said Kevin replied your request for prom date with an emphatic yes. Your answer pained me like a knife wound. I was devastated.

"I wasn't angry at you or Kevin, but I was mad at myself. I was mad at myself for my low self-esteem. I was mad that I couldn't express my feelings. I was mad that I missed my only chance to get close to the person I had a serious crush on. I was so shattered that I didn't want to go to prom. However, I was quickly reminded by my conscience that was not the right thing to do, and that I must be part of the event my friends and I worked so hard to put together.

"Please don't get me wrong...but for a short moment I grew jealous of you, seeing Kevin as your prom date. I wasn't sure if and when I would ever see Kevin again, so I kept staring at him. But after a while, I didn't see Kevin anymore. Instead I saw the result of my dread. All levees were broken at that moment and it troubled me so much that it was the final tipping point after which the avalanche of introspection has run amuck. I realized that if I did not overcome my fears, the tornado called 'fear' would devour everything in its way, and I would lose everything I ever longed for. After a few months of emotional turmoil, I came to conclusion that to stop shredding my life, I first need to shred fear from every cell in my body.

"I started college. I no longer missed Kevin. My determination to assuage my fears galvanized me, and I opted to study information systems and technology. Looking into the mirror and talking to myself wasn't helping me. It was then I met three wonderful friends who helped me in overcoming my fears. They encouraged and cheered me at every step, and I listened to them. They suggested I start simple, by writing blogs and responding to the comments, which were mostly anonymous. By doing that, I learned that everyone has their own opinion that comes from the emotional attachment they have to their preconceived notions and predisposed beliefs. And as long as my belief system is tenable and based on facts, I can support my coherent arguments. They then raised the exercise to the next level. They would throw in a discursive essay topic and give me a week to prepare for it. On Sundays, the three of them would empathetically listen to what I have to say, appreciate my thoughts, point out the flaws in my flaccid arguments, and then we'd have illuminating discussions.

"By doing that, I learned to put the best evidence on the table and that my inferences are only as strong as the assumptions which undergird them. Sometimes they would also surprise me by inviting a larger group. Soon, I no longer stammered. I gained confidence and started being vocal about my opinions. What I thought of as exercises to squash my fear of public speaking, also resulted in a byproduct: I became good at researching the topics and arriving at rigorous conclusions based on scientific facts.

"After three years of impassioned struggle and gradual progress, a wonderful thing happened to me in the form of a fortuitous encounter. I was attending a conference and I saw Kevin. He was working part-time for the event management company. After the conference, he complimented me for overcoming my social anxiety and for asking questions during the conference. Kevin told me that he was following my blog all these years and had also commented on several topics. He also confessed that he had feelings for me back in high school but since there was a lot going on in his personal life, he didn't express his liking. I guess I still had feelings for Kevin because I was blushing at everything he was telling me. I spent the rest of that day in the cafeteria with Kevin, which felt like a few seconds but were in fact a few hours.

"We met often after that accidental rendezvous. After graduation, Kevin and I started our own event management company that does parties and conferences for local businesses. In the course of time, our company became CK Production House where he takes care of the design, finances and logistics, and I take care of research, marketing and advertising."

Listening to Clarisse, I couldn't stop but to think how important it is to overcome our fears and work on our weaknesses. Her love for Kevin, and the reflection that she lost him because of her phobia had sparked a change. A great company of friends helped her in the process. But the most important thing was, she listened to them. Friends play a major role in our lives. Friends can make us or break us; they can be a blessing or blight. In my case, I abused my friendships by not listening to them. But Clarisse made the right decision.

Abi and Clarisse organized some games for children and some TV time which included animated cartoon shows from my high school days. A magic show was set up during the dinner time. As soon as the dinner was announced, all the kids started thumping and chanting "magic" in a perfect cadence. The magician was no amateur. Along with the kids, I was dazzled by his deft sleight of hand and perplexed to his legerdemain tricks that belied that the gimmicks were illusory. During the dinner, as men talked about crooked politics and their vacation plans, Audi talked about how Ethan and Abi are linchpins to SYMBIOSIS, and how their combined scientific acumen helps everyone at the company stay flying.

Karaoke, the penultimate event for the day followed the dinner. Songs were selected randomly from a medley, and, Abi being the best singer amongst us, started off by singing "Celebration" by Kool & the Gang. She killed the floor with her stellar voice. Next in line, Clarisse sang "Shake It Off" by Taylor Swift. I didn't know Clarisse could sing so well. She was amazing and nailed the song in consonant with the tunes. Audi was next. Audi sang "Funkytown – Lipps, Inc," and deftly matched her amplitude with the crescendo. The song was so catchy that we all started dancing to it.

After those wonderful performances, it was my turn. I had to sing Kelly Clarkson's "Stronger". I managed to finish the song, but with great dissonance between the lyrics and the music. I am definitely an inept singer. It was then Ethan's turn, and he had "Cheap Thrills" by Sia. Though singing is not his forte, I can say he tried his discordant best not to create total cacophony. Later, Sydney joined him, and we asked them to sing a duet. As they sang "All I Have" by Jennifer Lopez and LL Cool J, it felt like the sweetest euphony we'd heard thus far and it was so adorable to watch them sing together. Their love was in air and their eyes showed the feelings they have for each other.

Next up was the newly engaged couple. Fres dedicated "500 Miles" by The Proclaimers to Kelsey, and later they both sang "Dream a Little Dream of Me" by Ella Fitzgerald and Louis Armstrong. Everyone's ears were ready to listen to the next duet by Abi and her rockstar husband Adam. They sang "Up Where We Belong" by Joe Cocker and Jennifer Warnes. They were flawless. It sounded like the original singers performing.

Later, we all passionately insisted Adam sing few of his own compositions. Though most of us could just impulsively tap our feet and undulate to the rhythm of his sensual and soulful music, our master choreographer, Abigail, with her lithe and sinuous movements complemented her husband's music in perfect sync. We couldn't resist but to shout "Encore! Encore!" for a repeat performance. A few of us later moved on to Pictionary game. Audi, Sydney, Kelsey, Kevin, and Adam were part of one team, and Clarisse, Abi, Fres, Ethan and I were part of another team. After several rounds of neck-to-neck competition, the team I was in was finally declared the winner based on the aggregate score.

We lost track of time, but it was definitely very late by the time the adults dispersed to their respective rooms to relax and kickstart another beautiful day with the lovely people.

It was about 8AM on Sunday, December 16, 2029, the second and the last day of our reunion. Second day in a row, I was woken up by my phone ringing, but soon my eyes had a feast. The sunlight was refracting through the glass prisms installed at the window sill and was creating beautiful artificial rainbows in the room. The phone call was my parents, checking up on me.

As I walked into the ballroom by about 10AM, owing to our Christmas theme, there was Christmas allure all over the place. The get-together was planned to end after lunch, and all of us to diverge again and to reunite five years later in St. Louis, the result of the majority vote conducted the day before post-dinner from the three choices we were presented to select our next venue. I met many friends on Sunday who couldn't come the day before. Then walked in the parasite in human form, Tanya. Back in our high school days, Tanya was recognized as a renowned opportunist, and her wanton mother, Chelsea, had luminous appellation of being a promiscuous golddigger. We all saw Tanya following earnestly in her licentious mother's footsteps.

It appeared that Tanya came to the reunion for an ostentatious display and to flaunt her status. For the hour or so she stayed, she adulterated everyone's minds with diabolical thoughts. I had no idea what happened and the reason for enmity between Clarisse and Tanya, but I had to quell Clarisse to avoid a showdown. Undeniably, an abrasive person who takes pride in mentally maiming and denouncing everyone, Tanya took an aim at denigrating and undermining Audi's munificence for a brief moment. As I happened to overhear her egregious statement crafted from her cynical beliefs, Tanya told someone at the reunion that millionaires and billionaires know that people are not going to remember them as rich people, and the only reason why they largesse and undertake philanthropic activities is so that they will be remembered.

I was aghast at her temerity and appalled by the flagrant words that came out of her mouth to discredit Audi. But knowing Tanya, her brazen and impudent comments were because she has no regard for the ramifications of her actions and because she is a coward. Regardless if it is her foolishness or recklessness or shamelessness, there are few things in life that are irrevocable, and one of those that we cannot take back are the words that come out of our mouth. Tanya knew nothing about Audi. How can she judge her? How can anyone judge? Based on facts? Yes. But even with a vast body of hard facts, don't we deduce and conclude based on our beliefs and prejudices? Moreover, in reality, don't we tend not to care about finding the facts and make our opinions of others directly based on our notions? I guess that part of Tanya is in everyone as we gravitate towards typecasting people based on their professions, religions, and races.

We all took umbrage to Tanya's inflammatory remarks. Abi, known for her composure, fumed with anger after hearing Tanya's comments about Audi. I could see the fury in her face. What I assumed would be a barrage of invectives and expletives from Abi to counteract Tanya's attempts to defile Audi's reputation was ultimately just one angry, wordless stare. However it was, the stare worked and seemed to mortify Tanya, who left the reunion without bidding any goodbyes. I got suspicious that Abi probably knew a shady secret of Tanya's.

Just when we thought the bloodsucker was gone though, she returned with a wedding invitation. Though she left in disgrace, her return just mirrored her cynical attitude. The wedding invitation was flamboyant, and the wedding was in Italy. And in a way that embodied her character, Tanya was very particular to make sure none of us were wholeheartedly invited. We all could sense the sarcasm in her tone. But the tip of the iceberg was the groom. I was startled for a minute and my eyes dilated in shock. As it turned out, Tanya connived and successfully lured my ex-husband, Philip.

I couldn't think of any other person, even a parasite like Tanya, going through what I went through. I pulled Tanya aside and tried my best to persuade her not to proceed with her plans to marry Philip. After fervidly trying to sway her for over fifteen minutes, it became clear to me that even a fierce apex predator may give up on its prey, but Tanya is inexorable. I failed to dissuade her. It appeared that once she locked in her target, nothing could deter her from pursuing her victim. I gave up my efforts thinking that may be Tanya is Philip's punishment and is the nature's way for the order of things. All I could do then was to wish Tanya happiness with her married life, and I truly meant it.

Tanya came into our lives during tenth grade when her mother moved to Chicago. Initially we all thought she was a shy and timorous teenager as she didn't talk to anyone. But under the pretense of being shy, she was surveying everyone and not until one day when we saw her going out with a senior did it become clear to us. A few months later, the senior came looking for Tanya and she ignored him. We all smelled the rotten fish and surmised that something was wrong. But it took us few more of such incidents to realize that Tanya is tactful in constantly changing her friends and her interests. It became a common practice for her to get close to boys who were rich or popular. She was a shallow sycophant and toady who can blandish anyone with flattery. Armed with a glib, manipulative tongue that works only to fulfil her wishes, she will treat them as trash as soon as her purpose is fulfilled. And as if her genes were mutated to Chicago's weather, she went from fully opaque clothed in the tenth grade to dressing provocatively in diaphanous clothing, and ultimately bagging an unofficial title for Scantily Clad Student by the final year of high school.

I watched in wonder when Tanya left in disgrace after just one look from Abi. I got curious to know Abi's supernatural power. As Abi revealed when asked, it was that in the final year of high school, Tanya's focus shifted to Kevin, the most popular, handsome and delicious boy in school. But Kevin was also intelligent. Tanya needed a bait to get close to him. Clarisse, who already had a crush on Kevin, became her toy. Knowing Clarisse's social anxiety, Tanya, dissembling her true motives, approached her and offered to help. Under the guise of "helping" Clarisse, Tanya started talking to Kevin. Crafty and conniving, she told Kevin exactly what he needed to hear to show pity on her.

Tanya was being a double agent. To Clarisse, she said she was doing it all for her. But in reality, she'd found her next victim. Tanya acted so credible that she earned Clarisse's trust and used her drawbacks to her full advantage. But Kevin, having seen more of life than anyone has, was not a typical teenager to fall for Tanya's cloying lines, could see through her and never entertained her.

The only person who could see through the cloud was Abi. And the only way for Abi to get that leech off Kevin and to help Clarisse was to make Tanya realize that Kevin is not wealthy. With that news, Tanya was dismayed that she wasted her time on Kevin. Though discontented with her failure, nevertheless with an unfettered hope, Tanya moved on to her next target. But before moving on to her next victim, she devilishly went to Clarisse and told her scurrilous lies she weaved about Kevin. She told Clarisse that Kevin was not into her and in fact hates her. But Abi, knowing everything that happened, made it clear to Clarisse that everything that Tanya said were lies, and to help her, Abi selected both Clarisse and Kevin into the prom committee.

After I heard what Tanya did to Clarisse in high school, it became clear to me why Clarisse got angry seeing Tanya, and why I had to subdue her. But I was wrong. Something more happened after the high school. As Clarisse said, "Even after all the dishonesty, I forgave Tanya because it was my mistake to seek her help knowing her character. I didn't think it was correct to blame her for my defects. But something that was beyond my control resulted in a hapless encounter with her after the high school. She too got admission in Georgia Tech, and I saw firsthand how she toyed with three hearts simultaneously. Those three hearts were my friends who helped me overcome my fears. While, I saw three good friends in them, Tanya saw an opportunity to exploit them.

"Tanya certainly has all the evil qualities in her, but there is patently one great quality in her; she is an Oscar worthy charlatan. She effortlessly can play several cunning roles to get her victim's attention. With Tom, she played a helpless and innocent girl to lean over his shoulder. With John, she played the 'homesick' card. John is such a caring person that he would escort me back to my apartment after work to protect me like a bodyguard. I never asked him to escort me, he just did it out of the goodness of his heart. Later John bought a secondhand, rundown car and he would give me a ride home. But after Tanya started playing the lonely, homesick, nostalgic card, John would take her on long drives to alleviate her fake wistfulness.

"But soon, Tanya dumped John when she found someone with a new BMW. My third friend, Harry, was her personal ATM. She owed, and probably still owes Harry a lot of money. Harry is a genius and toiled his way to a research assistant which paid him well. Every time she needed money, she went to Harry. Tanya is so shrewd and wily that she didn't directly ask for it. She created situations such that Harry would voluntarily offer to help. When I read the history of several civilizations that had stories of a single woman bringing down even the kings to their knees, I didn't believe them. But that is what happened right in front of my eyes. All three of my friends developed feelings for Tanya and fantasized that she was also loving them back. Tanya must have performed some kind of sorcery because it was as if they were all in some kind of a hallucinatory trance. I knew her well, so I warned them, but my lectures to my friends that she is an insidious woman with a devil behind her veneer of innocence didn't work. My sermons were rejected. Then, one by one, slowly woke up from the reverie after Tanya rebuffed their proposals and moved on to her next victim.

"The story of my three good friends was actually the inspiration for our first youth educational video series. In fact, the success of CK productions actually came from that video in which we gave a message to all the young boys and girls that anytime a person doesn't give you a closure and talks to you tangentially or only when they want something from you, stay away from them."

It was no wonder why I had to constrain Clarisse from physically handling and defacing Tanya. Such toxic stories are not only somber, but also makes us enervated. And clearly, Tanya is a testament to an archetypal image that the weak people are the most treacherous of all. Tanya's story also made it clear to me that there exists a bait for every person who just cannot resist gobbling, except I guess for a resolute person.

We were so much drawn into the conversation that we didn't realize it was past lunch time. The lunch menu was extensive and though I grew a little hungry and weary, I was abstemious and temperate in subtly devouring the dishes.

ABIGAIL

I also met several of my classmates. While some of them were my close friends from my bullying gang, most of them were just acquaintances. One of them was Samir. After earning his Master's in Mechanical Engineering, he started as a mechanical design engineer in an automobile company. Though the job paid well, it far satisfied his creativity. After attending the ten-year high school reunion in 2024, he decided to turn his hobby into a profession. His hobby was art. I still have the caricature he made of me back in high school. Samir now teaches art classes for middle and high school students and conducts summer camps for aspiring artists. And still working in the same automobile company, he now designs car exteriors so that they look exotic while simultaneously reducing the aerodynamic drag forces and maximizing the interior passenger space. As his parents supported his childhood hobby financially and emotionally, he now basically employed his hobby to make money for his survival.

Kris, only a few years ago, completed his residency and started working as a neurosurgeon. I was amazed to discover how long and grueling it is to start a career as a doctor.

Becky chose to be a fashion designer. Because of the western prodigal lifestyle of spending exorbitant amount of time and money on weddings, it came as a no wonder to me as to why she chose to specialize in wedding dresses.

Robyn, after earning her degree in Aviation and Pilot Training, started working as a commercial pilot and then as an airline pilot. The flight I was on from Chicago to Phoenix on Thursday was indeed piloted by Robyn. She was the flight captain. Though her stay at the reunion was short, I managed to ask her what it is like to be a pilot. She said, "Flying has always been my passion. When I am in the cockpit flying the plane, the view of the sky gives me a new perspective on life. All of life's troubles shrink down and appear small. Though my job description just says that I am responsible to take passengers from Point A to Point B safely, I always believed it is more than that. It is being accountable to lives of complete strangers who trust the airlines."

As the reunion came to an end, we all hugged each other and took an embarrassing number of pictures. Though we took many pictures with the technology, I will always cherish the image I took from my heart.

In about two hours, I was back in Phoenix. Before heading to the airport, Ethan and I decided to make a quick stop at Abi's beautiful home. Ethan, like my father, is old-fashioned and prefers to drive the car himself instead of using the self-driving mode. While he was driving, he asked me how long I have known Abigail. I thought he already knew the answer. But I guess I didn't leave him any other topic to talk about as I embargoed talking about my personal life.

Well, I'd known Abi and her family since I was about five years old. There is something idiosyncratic with the Roy Family. They have an aura, a positive vibe around them. To start with, I never saw Mr. Roy without his benevolent smile. He was the most popular and cherished person in our neighborhood. He used to give free football coaching during the weekends to all the children in a nearby park. No, not American football. The real football. Yes, soccer. He had a unique way of coaching. The ball was small, half the size of the standard football, and heavy. Though there were always enough players, the teams were never the full size and the circumscribed area of the soccer field was extremely small by all standards. Some coaches and professional players mocked and derided at his implausible method, but kids would pour in from miles away to train under his unique system. He would encourage kids to make mistakes and would even reward them for making errors. It was as if his coaching principle is 'mistake-focused' practice. Except for the effort, I never saw him making any laudatory remarks. Except when players think that they should not risk making mistakes, I never saw him decry or admonish anyone. Like Abi, Mr. Roy talks a lot. But more than ninety percent of his words are pure information. And what we do and how we use that information is up to us.

Mrs. Roy, an eminent scholar and a psychology professor, is equally prominent and driven as Mr. Roy. In addition to raising three children, she found time to write books on the art of persuasion and the psychology of human relationships.

Just then, Ethan got a call from Sydney. To give them some privacy, I quickly put on my earbuds to listen to some music, but I couldn't help but think about the sisters trio "RAY" - Regina, Abigail, and Yeva. The three sisters were special in every way. And it is not just Abi, all three of them have effervescent personality, and they all got the same infectious smile from their dad. For starters, they never fight, which itself is uncanny. They are so close to each other that they never needed an outside "BFF". And while no one would classify any of the trio as their BFF either, they were friendly with everyone. The whole family is brainy; it is as if their parents failed to inoculate them against the disease and they all became infected with intelligence. In fact, it was when Abigail won the National Spelling Bee Championship during her middle school, that's when I gave her the nickname, 'Brainiac'. They are jack of all trades and well, master of many. They can make intelligent discussions about anything around the globe. One can talk to them about science, technology, history- not just American, but of the several human civilizations that still exist and once prevailed the world. Being an orthodox family, all three sisters were trained in Indian classical dance and music. They are very independent, strong-willed and steadfast. And what enthralled me was, topics that seem to normal people as a 'TED Talk', is their typical dinner table dialogue.

To me personally, Abigail is a paradox. She always manifested herself as a confluence of opposing attributes. She is tough but soft and sensitive, brainy but humorous and silly, talkative but composed and demure, generous but realistic and practical. Such was her ebullient personality that she is the embodiment of helping, caring, loving, inquisitive, extrovert, witty, ambitious, reliable, authoritative, brave, observant, systematic, and a ton of other positive virtues. Her popularity was such that everyone adored her, not because that she won the National Spelling Bee Championship, but because of her affable and amiable character. Yet boys were a bit scared and didn't have the courage to confess and express their attraction to her. She did the right things at the right time, all the time. An honor roll student, Abi had always been adept at managing time among her passions such as dance, music and art. She became an all-rounder talented in innumerable ways.

She always kept us updated with her sisters' lives, but the last I knew about them was back in 2018. Regina finished her theater and fine arts degree and was pursuing directing films and documentaries on real world problems. Yeva, a year younger to Abi and the apple of everyone's eyes, is very matured and super tough. She was a soccer player and was aspiring to play in the World Cup.

As I was driving down the memory lane, Ethan drove us to Abi's beautiful home. The home was all decked up with Christmas decorations. Adam's moms helped to decorate their house, said Ethan. They were visiting Abi's place for Christmas. The home was as welcoming as the people inside it were and is elegantly decorated with homemade craftwork. Every inch of the house was ornate and screaming "Live, Love and Laugh". Undoubtedly, Adam's moms have a good taste in picking the colors.

We passed by Adam's office before heading to the living room. It had everything he loves: pictures of his family and large weighty tomes on one side, and keyboard and guitar on the other side. Apparently, he still plays and writes songs for his kids. As I walked into the kitchen blindly following the aroma of freshly baked muffins, my eyes had a carnival watching the CRO of a multi-billion-dollar company baking in an apron. The banana muffins were yummy, rivaling that of my mom's recipe. In addition, the antiseptic kitchen seemed to compete with semiconductor fabrication cleanroom. The kitchen appeared fit to eat off anything from any surface without following any five- or ten-second rule. Abi has always been a great cook, but it had been ages since I ate her food. With one glance through the cabinets, I was sure that the preponderance of spices in Abi's spice rack was more extensive than her clothes and shoes in the wardrobe combined.

I also came to know about Adam and his beautiful mothers. They reminded me of my parents. Adam is their only son. I heard about their struggle for their legal identity and how they patiently waited for the courts to decide in their favor. Finally, they married in Massachusetts. The older Adam grew, the stronger he felt the agony of his parents to be accepted as a couple. That inspired Adam to study law and help people in need and despair. Though he was determined to get his license and practice law, he loved music. Law was his heart, but music was his soul. And just as every singer has a unique personality, Adam's music comes from the agonized depths of his soul to disseminate joy and to touch other's souls.

Hearing about Adam's moms' struggles to be recognized as a couple inevitably brought me to an essential question. What is the most fundamental and paramount criteria to get married, of course throwing the constitutional and religious convictions aside. Love and respect for each other, or being opposite genders?

Undeniably, the requirement should be love and respect. While, judging a person in my opinion is immoral, and though we are never in a position to judge, we typically get judgmental anytime we see anyone who doesn't think, speak or look like us. Though our sensory organs are the first ones to notice things that are different from us, and we like to think that it is our brain that makes the judgement, it is actually our character that makes the decision. A good character understands and helps, doesn't judge.

By the way, who gets to decide what is normal and what isn't? And on what basis? One's conscientious beliefs? I wish I could tell everyone that,

Just because one's color is different than yours doesn't give you the right to oppress.
Just because one speaks a different language than you do doesn't make you smarter.
Just because one has different religious beliefs than yours, doesn't give you the right to judge their faith.
And just because one has a different sexual orientation than yours doesn't give you the right to take away their liberty to live happily and peacefully.

Just look at your hand. Are all fingers the same height and width? The answer is NO. If your own hand doesn't have fingers that look the same, how can you expect the people to look like you and have the same opinions as you do? Just because the opposable thumb is different from the rest of the fingers doesn't make it useless or worthless. Try picking up a paper from the table without using your thumb. If the remaining four fingers started bullying the thumb for its appearance and its place on the hand, then thumb can just smile and say, "If I weren't there, you wouldn't be able to eat, open a bottle cap, pull up your blanket while you sleep, or even tear a paper. I may not be the only useful finger, but you would need me as much as you need the rest."

I could only empathize with Adam's mom's feelings and the pain they endured to just be together. But at the same time, it remained an enigma to me that we could grasp the intricate laws of physics, explore the counterintuitive ideas of the 'big bang', and unlock the secrets from the farthest reaches of the cosmos to the smallest atomic particles, viruses and bacteria; yet no amount of investment and education seem to elicit the mysterious secrets of the inveterate and the irrational nature of human prejudice.

As I walked through the morning room, which should be aptly named "The Selfie Room", I noticed a selfie of Abigail's whole family: RAY, Mr. and Mrs. Roy, Adam and his moms, and all of RAY's kids. Curious about Abi's sisters, I inquired about them. Regina became a director and now lives in Los Angeles, California. Her recent work was "80 and Not Out", based on eighty years post-independent India that is still going strong preserving its several thousands of years of cultural heritage and civilization, the enduring struggle, and the cultural juxtaposition between the older generation trying to dodge and the younger generation trying to espouse the influence of the Western culture. Abi mentioned that the documentary received worldwide commendation and was also screened at multiple international film festivals. Yeva played in the team representing the United States in the 2019 women's soccer World Cup. With Yeva on the team and with a high level of camaraderie among the athletes, United States had a facile victory and won the most coveted world champions title. She later retired due to a career ending knee injury. Even after the debacle that ended her soccer career, she didn't adamantly adhere and obsess over her longing to be the best player, nor felt that her future and the opportunities were desiccated. She actively created an opportunity and became the top sports analyst in the country.

I was sure that Mr. and Mrs. Roy are very proud of their efforts to raise three strong women. They truly were a 'RAY' of courage, success and happiness. In addition to soccer coaching, Mr. Roy would also give us guidance quotations on several matters, though none of the kids used to pay much attention to them. I still remember two such phrases. The first one is, "Communication is the key to understanding". Abi once told me that Mr. Roy creates a list of the monthly expenses and shares it with rest of the family so that everyone in the family knew how much they earned and how much they were spending. It was a simple but brilliant idea of communication to make children respect money and educate them how difficult it is to earn money than to spend it.

The second one was, "Understanding and trust are the keys to success". It is absolutely true whether regarding family or work. Though one needs to first build trust with anyone outside the family, families are born with innate love and deep-rooted trust as their intrinsic quality. As most teenagers do, I told my parents many lies and later accused them of not trusting their own daughter. But the RAY trio never gave a reason not to trust, and as a result everyone earned the privilege to explore anything they want. Though RAY were given the freedom, they knew it was the most expensive gift and that they could not abuse it. One such caution I witnessed was during prom night. The party was running late and Abi, being one of the organizers, couldn't leave early. While I was throwing up outside, Abi called her parents to let them know that she was running late. It was a simple gesture of updating them on her safety, but also served to retain the trust. Myself on the other hand, I always ignored my parents' requests to inform them where I was going. And on the prom night, though Kevin kept badgering me to leave, I never informed my parents that I was running late. When Kevin dropped me home late from the prom, despite my furtive attempts to enter the house, he had to weather a colossal load of verbal insults and upbraiding when my dad unleashed an angry diatribe on him because of me.

Each member of Abi's family was an open book. They had no secrets among them. Parents could see what the kids were doing, and kids were allowed to talk about anything with the parents.

I felt so nostalgic after remembering Abi's parents that I asked her to do a video call. Mr. and Mrs. Roy were retired and on world tour with Regina. Mr. Roy answered, and he looked the same as I always remembered him with his classic smile. He still remembered me and before I could say hello, he took over and asked how my parents and I were doing.

The weather was so nice that Adam was playing with his children in the backyard. The more I learned about Abi's family, I got a nagging question in my brain that only Adam could answer - Why did he give up his music career? And how did switching careers work out? As Adam explained, "A year after we got married, we had our first child, Alisa. I was out of the country on a scheduled tour and Abi delivered Alisa earlier than expected. I couldn't be with her for the delivery. After Alisa was born, things got very busy for me and I barely spent time with them. That's when I decided to take a break from music and stay home so that Abi could continue her work.

"Later when Alisa started preschool, we decided to use my law background and set up a home office as a legal counselor. Initially, I had qualms about switching the profession, but I am now really content with my legal career. Over the years, I learned human psychology from Abi's mom which helped me enter a person's mind and heart. As I gained basic insights into the human nature and deep understanding of how our brains work, I also discovered that the true function of a lawyer is to unite both parties riven asunder, and to seek a win-all solution by serving the best interests of both parties. As years passed by, we had our second child, Asher. We named him after my band."

Adam and Abi's story deepened and amplified my faith in love. They always supported each other's decision and opinions. In the process, I learned a lot more about love. Love makes us to do the ultimate sacrifice, self-sacrifice. Adam surrendered his career in music so that Abi could have a career. I cannot think of any other sacrifice that is more proof of true love. I also learned that love is not just the driving force in a relationship. Maybe love is the paramount parameter for getting married, but respect takes over when one is in relationship. Emotionally invested marriage has mutual respect for each other. In fact, as long as one has respect for the other, one will have a successful married life, because respect helps to preserve love. I lauded Adam's courage to propose to Abi.

Abi is so lovely, yet intimidating and totally focused on myriad of passions, not in a million years would I have guessed she would fall in love. But after talking with Adam, I became sure it was Adam's character, not his music that melted Abi. But I wondered, though she is brilliant, if she even knew that she was falling in love.

I was still not sure when and how Abi decided to become good at everything. It could just be in her family culture as everyone in their family are brainy. Of course, no one is born a prodigy. Everyone is born with same innate instincts - hunger, fear, desire, to name a few; everything else is what we decide to become. Genius is grown and that is what both Audi and Abi did. They were not born different. All I can deduce is, when Audi decided to change, genius didn't touch her. Her thinking profoundly changed and she decided to struggle and labor, which made all the difference.

My last stop in the journey of Abi's love story was their wedding photos and videos. It was clear that the ceremony was no less than a royal wedding, of course, minus the superfluous expenses. They had their wedding in both Indian and American styles. Unlike my wedding, everyone from Abi's family was present, dancing and having fun. Though I didn't understand any of the Indian songs, I found myself spontaneously tapping my feet as an involuntary reflex to the beats. From all the years I had known her, she never wore any makeup. But in her wedding, Abi looked much different with a coating of maquillage and serpentine looking intricately convoluted labyrinthine red tattoos on her hands. As I left Abi's home with a good feeling, I wished Abi's life to be always filled with joy and happiness.

As Ethan and I started our drive to the airport, I realized that it is Abi's sagacity that enabled her to prosper both in her personal life and in her professional life, while maintaining and renewing a balance between the two acts under constant pressures and exigent demands. As life has become complex, stressful and exhausting, a productive and meaningful life is a delicately well-balanced act of effective professional life with joyful personal life. Careers are often demanding, and we do have the proclivity to excel professionally in the competitive environment. As a result, after being immersed ourselves for long hours at work, we cannot just disconnect ourselves from work. And in the world of smart gadgets and technology at the fingertips, we constantly do our office work, either physically or mentally.

While we have the penchant to shine professionally, it is also equally important to have a life outside of work in such a way that personal and professional life are in harmony. Everyone gets the same amount of time in a day; it depends on the individual how they apportion and allocate time on things that matters them the most. Though is impossible not to think about family at work, and work when with family, if a person is enjoying everything they do, then they are living in an equilibrium. However, when either work or family/friends adds stress, then they are no longer living in concord. I always see work and personal life as being on the either side of the balance with the fulcrum as me standing somewhere in the middle. When the gravity of work pulls us down, we must counterbalance the life with a commensurate push from family and friends, and vice-versa. This push and pull will hold our life in dynamic equilibrium. Unfortunately, there is no single formula that would work for everyone, but fortunately there is also no right or wrong endeavor as one has to figure out what works best for them to reach their equilibrium. I guess it is just like some mothers prefer co-sleeping with their infants and some mothers prefer to have separate room; there is no right or wrong. My suggestion to anyone is to follow Fres's advice: we should be able to look ourselves in the mirror every night and be truthful and honestly say, "Whatever the equilibrium I reached by promoting and relegating the priorities, it's the best one for me and my family."

RN1729

I completely lost track of time while watching Abi's wedding videos. Ethan rushed me to the airport, but I forced him to turn on the self-driving mode to reach on time. It was the evening of Sunday, December 16, 2029, and I was on my flight back home to Chicago, hoping to be home before my kids went to sleep and be able to kiss them good night. But my mind was still roaming the reunion.

Over the last several years, I realized the treasure of family relationships and learned a lot about how we value money if we earned it through hard work. Also, having interacted and personally associated with multifarious people and acquainted with their quirks, I can say for sure that the paramount and preeminent trait of a human being is their 'character'. It doesn't matter how bad a person's English or their communications skills are, their character and integrity speaks volumes. When I went in for the interview on Friday, my mission was simply to get the job, make some extra money to raise my family well, and start a career with new challenges. Given the most important attribute is the character, I questioned if a person's character could be tested in an interview. I concluded that it could not and reasoned that it would be the rationale for why employers ask for character references during the interview. Accordingly, I made my personality such that my communication skills and my attitude were *the* weapons in my mission, and knew my references would speak for my character.

In addition to an exhilarating feeling I had after meeting, connecting and socializing with my old friends, the last two days had also been a great learning experience. First, I learned that character and personality are two inseparable traits and are tightly interwoven into the fabric we call humanity. In fact, our character governs and regulates how we speak

148

and inspire others. In a nutshell, how we communicate and make others feel with our words gives away what our character is.

Though I was excited to attend my first high school reunion, my expectations were low. I assumed that everyone would be there to flaunt their status and job titles, and that the social gathering would be simply vapid and insipid. I even questioned myself – "Why would one need to meet anyone in person, given all the AR and VR technology at our fingertips?" But there are definitely few things that technology can never supplant, and one of them is the vibes we get when we connect interpersonally with others.

First from Clarisse, I learned that fear, anxiety, and apprehension are always present in the course of life, in one fashion or other. But the one who flourishes is the one who releases their inhibition and takes a dive. Fear is a common ingredient in life, affecting everyone. But "fear" is a big umbrella of emotions. It can make us or break us. One type of fear that comes from our ignorance can easily make us cowards. Because of this toxic fear, people reject themselves before even taking a chance at the first step. This type of destructive fear basically holds oneself hostage. It is an absolute block to progress and a vicious killer. We also let this toxic fear cumulate in our mind so much that it gets more detrimental than the actual situation. Unfortunately, there is no magic bullet to dodge this trepidation. Over the years, I have seen many people get depressed and shrink in this noxious emotion, and avoiding struggles without realizing that we actually grow from the experiences of conquering and get better. I guess the cure to cease to let this fear control is by asking for help, and getting the emotional support from family and friends or trusted people. Another type of fear is the innocuous fear, which instead of paralyzing, energizes us. This motivating fear helps us to force ourselves towards our goals and allows us to grow. While appreciation and recognition are fundamental motivators, the innocuous fear is an all-powerful motivator because a person who is feared will do anything.

Roadblocks, hindrances, setbacks and obstacles are also common on the path to success. In fact, every one of us, rich or poor, goes through barriers in our lives. Ethan encountered an impediment in his dream of doing a Ph.D. when his mom was diagnosed with cancer. He had to take a brief hiatus and a detour while attaining his dream, but he got back on track with his goal of guiding young researchers and teaching students. Though roadblocks throw us into predicaments, a positive attitude is taking those signals as an indicator for an alternate way to explore the dream. It is not those roadblocks and setbacks but rather our response to those obstacles that reveals and defines us. We really do not know what we truly are if only wonderful things keep happening to us. In fact, it is during adversity that a person learns more about themselves. Hindrances challenge our thinking. Most of the time, there is a way to cut through and solve the toughest problems we face. It's all in our mindset. And quite literally, there is no spice and excitement without those challenges in life.

I knew I was going to meet some old friends and some new people during the course of the reunion. One of those previously unfamiliar people was Sydney. Sydney taught me that 'change' is the fundamental constant in life. It is natural that in life we go through incessant cycles composed of inescapable periods of stability and change. Though intuitively we become aware of this ceaseless cycle once we reach adulthood, instinctively we still resist change as if it is our innate human nature. We even try to block the change because it feels like a daunting task of starting life all over again regardless of if the change was triggered by a good event or a bad event. Though vicissitudes in life are unavoidable, we detest change. The very idea of change makes us feel uncomfortable. Evolution has got a lot to teach us here as it has shown us the inevitable fate of the immutable species which failed to bend. Adaptation to change is needed for survival and progress. In fact, our potential to be mutable, ability to see opportunities and positives in the change, and in the dexterous handling of change lies the secret to our survival. I guess the only way to ensure change doesn't catch us off guard is for one to adjust their mentality to accept the fact that nothing is permanent, to always anticipate change, and quickly adapt to the change while embracing it because "change" doesn't give a damn about one's reasons. Still, even in the face of continuous blows of change, one's greatness lies in always progressing towards their life's purpose. A purpose in life is essential because our life is like a tortuous roller coaster, loop after loop, until we perish. With a purpose in life, we will enjoy and also show others how to relish the roller coaster. But those without a life's purpose, they just see ups and downs while living a dreary life just waiting for the end. Some of them may even get scared and jump out of the loop like Mort did on his eighteenth birthday.

Though my direct interaction with Audi was minimal, there were several things I learned from her. What Audi's dad told her before starting the company regarding leadership is also true in personal life.

We should always keep our word. Otherwise, we should not promise. While the right words from any person are good to hear, the same words from the right person are more effective. And what makes the person right is, keeping the promises by following up with actions until one gets the results. Building trust and respect is a lifelong process. But losing that same respect and admiration takes a fraction of a second. And once people lose trust in you, once they realize that they cannot count on you, you lose their respect, which is tantamount to death. Your principles make who you are and how you will be remembered. Though it is awful to lose billions, it's much worse to lose a good name. Nothing can undo a disgraced reputation and misplaced trust.

I also learned from Audi that like happiness, success is also subjective and means a lot of different things to different people. But most importantly, success is what we define it clearly by a specific criteria, and not by others. During high school, when Audi competed in several contests and never won any, I derided and made fun of her. But she savored success in every competition because she set her own goal and went up against that goal. Undeniably, the definition of success is deeply relative and personal so much that for example, while it might seem as an insignificant feat for many, making a good pair of shoes is a celebrated success for a cobbler. But one thing is clear—great people do not measure success by how much money one earned, but by how many failures one endured with smile and how many problems one encountered with courage to reach their goal. Similarly, a leader is not someone who brings success, but a leader is someone who inspires. Likewise, an exemplary leadership is not about a strong courageous leader who delivers success, but it is about how many failures the leader took in and how many triumphs the leader voluntarily awarded to others.

From Radha, I learned that the driving force behind the high achievers and the progress of humankind has been through reasoning and curiosity. As a child and as a teenager, we were always curious and ask the 'why' questions such as, "Why do I have to tell everything that happened in school every day?", "Why is it called *Mother Nature* and not *Father Nature*?", and sometimes not so fatuous questions such as, "Why should I do anything good when the world is bad to me?" But as we reach the adulthood, only a select few continue asking the 'why' questions. Radha's story also brought me to a conclusion that a person's behavior tells a lot about their upbringing. For example, a dancer. If a dancer does well, the praise goes to the dancer. But when the dancer doesn't perform well, the blame goes to the dance teacher that the teacher did not train well. In a similar way, a person's execrable behavior automatically tells a lot about the person's parents, their teachers, and the culture in which they were raised.

Though we are the authors of our destiny, clearly a big elephant in the integral equation of our life is our friends. It is well-known universally that we eventually become the people we hang out with. Friends and people we spend time with influence our thinking, behavior, actions, and sooner or later, our future. This is absolutely true if we hang out with bad company as I saw what happened with Doyle. And if you are in the company of such pernicious people, often called as toxic people, there is no better time in future than now to stop being with them. Even if you haven't set your goals as yet, or aren't working towards your goals, you are still better off spending your time alone with a good book than spending time with toxic people. If you don't, one day, the cancer that is waiting to happen will wake up from quiescent state and will wreak havoc in your life. It is said not to judge a book by its cover, but a person will definitely be judged by his or her friends. But whether we become the people we hang out with also depends on how motivated we are for the change. I was encompassed in good company of Ethan, Abi and Audi all through my high school and college. But I never became like them because I didn't have the motivation. Clarisse, on the other hand, had that desire and ambition.

A lot is usually voiced about motivation, but I discovered that there are two types of motivation: intrinsic and extrinsic motivation. While intrinsic motivation comes from within, extrinsic motivation comes from outside sources and usually out of necessity. While with internal motivation we are willing to go out of our comfort zone on our own will and ready to face any obstacles and challenges, external motivation is transient and dissipates over time requiring recurrent external stimuli.

In the process of stimulating interaction with my friends in the convivial atmosphere of the reunion, I also learned a lot more about the essential constituents of human life such as passion, interest, and inspiration. Though there is no doubt that every person will have their own definition for each of those abstract terms, one thing became clear to me that we are not born with a pre-determined passion(s). We develop passions. Radha had developed her passion for cooking. Audi, influenced by the science fiction books she read, developed her passion for space exploration. We all have several passions during childhood, such as dancing, singing, baseball, or basketball. By the time we reach adulthood, we may still have a passion for several things, but we don't follow up on each of those. Some people think they have passion for baseball. But after seeing an eighty mile per hour fastball, they give up. Some people have passion for bodybuilding and six-pack abs. But after following a strict diet and exercise for one or two months, they give up. It's not that there aren't any professional baseball players or bodybuilders, and it's also not that all those that gave up did not have the ardor or passion. Just having passion for something is not enough or sufficient. Passion, unaccompanied by enduring effort and perseverance is next to nothing. One needs a whole-hearted, unwavering commitment and hard work towards the goal or objective, and never be willing to give up regardless of the obstacles one faces. Otherwise, it would just be a momentary interest and cannot be called a true passion. Simply put, a person just interested finds excuses to not to sweat, and because of not being serious will remain a dilettante; whereas a person passionate for something does it no matter what it takes.

But let us not be misguided by the ferocity of the words. Dreams or incendiary passion does not exert any force. They just speak to our heart. It is through our mind that we need to put them to work so that they can provide a constant and everlasting push from within. And one other thing to keep in mind is that people follow their passions primarily because it provides a psychological satisfaction, not always monetary. But if one is clever enough, one can also make money from their passion. Almost everything invented and discovered in the world so far has happened not because they can make lots of money, but because they have passion for it. And because of the passion, we have researchers working tirelessly for years to find vaccines, and cures for cancers and other diseases. The term 'passion' could be best explained by an example. Suppose there are two people: Person A and Person B. Both are right-handed. But Person A decides, out of curiosity, to become ambidextrous. It may take a week to get used to brush teeth with the left hand, two weeks to unlock the door, a month to get used to the computer mouse, six months to drive the car, and a year or more to be able to write legibly with the left hand. Whereas Person B, out of necessity, say due to an injury, had to use left hand for every task. Not a day goes by that the Person B curses the injury, eagerly waiting to start using the right hand again. Though the difficulty is the same for both, Person A would do it with a smile because of passion. Passion is so omnipotent that if one has the true passion, they would not notice if they were practicing a skill in a derelict dungeon or a castle, or if it is scorching hot or shivering cold outside. True passion also shows up in how one respects their instructor.

As for inspiration, I learned that inspiration can come from several different sources. Inspiration can flare up from within oneself at any age, or anytime through a tragedy, or even by embarrassment. Audi is a prime example of getting self-inspired at an early age. Those few words of wisdom that Audi's dad spoke to her acted as a catalyst and stimulated her purpose in life. Her passion and curiosity further fueled her lifelong learning. Sydney's tragic loss of her sister was the source of her inspiration. Though it may seem weird, inspiration can develop through the feelings of inferiority or insecurity, and through a deep sense of self-embarrassment, whether it is personal or public shame. Some people need to see or hear other people who achieved the great to kindle that fire and get ignited. This type of ignition, usually seen in sports and in students, makes them say, "I can do this too", "I can achieve it too", "I can beat the mark", or "I can do it better". As for the public shame, which is decently called competition or rivalry, there is no better example than the United States stepping up its game in space exploration back in 1960s. The successful launch of "Sputnik", the first manmade object to reach space in 1957, sparked fear in Americans that the United States was falling behind the Soviets in technological capability. This feat gave prestige to the Soviet Union, and humiliation to other nations, which instigated and inspired the United States to kick the space race into the next gear. This, along with the achievement of the Soviet Union's sending the first man into space in 1961, has instigated and galvanized the United States to put a man on the moon by the end of 1960s, and simultaneously showed that no task is formidable enough for our will and the term "impossible" is only an opinion, and not a universal fact.

In addition, an incontrovertible fact is that inspiration can come at any age and in any position in life. There is no age limit to get inspired and to take an action. For example, at the age of 45, J. R. R. Tolkien began writing *The Lord of the Rings*, one of the bestselling fantasy adventure novels ever written. It took 12 years to write and was not fully published until Tolkien was 63 years old. Inspiration can also strike at several different times in life and one may be inspired to do something that is completely different from what they have been doing so far, such as how Samir changed his career from engineering to art.

But any load of passion and any volume of inspiration is nothing but building castles in the air if there is no indomitable will and commitment to supplement and fortify the gallant desire. With just a few words hitting the right spot, a spark was initiated, and Audi got ignited. She perpetuated the blaze, which eventually became a conflagration, and using the fuel of commitment, she decided on a life's purpose. So, the most important thing is, regardless of the source and magnitude of the spark and the ferocity of the initial storm, if there is no fuel within us, we cannot sustain that stimulus.

It is no surprise that none of my friends destined it as their aim in life to accumulate money. In our materialistic world we need money to survive, but it is egregious that some people equate success with money. In mathematics, we learn that a million examples do not prove a theory, but only one example is enough to disprove a theorem. If success equal to amassing money is the theorem, history is ripe with examples to disprove the theorem and I can quickly think of two: Mahatma Gandhi and Mother Teresa. Mahatma Gandhi was a common man with no political power and no wealth. Mother Teresa was no princess. She was poor, and she served the poor, dying, diseased and destitute. Yet, empires bowed to them and the funeral of these common people, who lived the life of greatest simplicity, was attended by queens, dignitaries and presidents of countries from all over the world.

Every one of my friends also went through a sour time in their life. Most of us spend our childhood in a protective cocoon that is built from our parents love, teenage years in our wildest imagination, and adulthood chasing after money. Until an emotional wound rips us open, we will not embrace our humanity. While that emotional injury could be as bad as my story, it nevertheless is the "Cambrian explosion" of our life. I walked into troubles and endured hardship because of my flaws. When we are in the midst of our suffering, we don't put ourselves in other person's shoes and we wrongly think that we are the only one in pain. We even grill ourselves as to why I am being punished. But the cruel truth is that, though the details differ, everyone's life is fraught with problems, difficulties, obstacles and tragedies. Just as the misery I created for myself from my foolishness, sometimes we, ourselves, are the reason we get into troubles, and other times it is completely out of our control like the sorrow that knocked Sydney's door. Though the bitter pain could come in any fashion (greed, gun, cancer, Doyle, addiction…etc), what I learned is that all that matters is how we come out of it and the mindset with

It's all about the decisions we make

which we come out of it. When we pass through the tunnel of caustic grief and pain, we can come out weaker, bitter and defeated, or stronger, better and with a new flame.

It is said that human beings are the product of nature and nurture, but we always forget about free will - the freedom to use our own discretion in our response to the problems. Clarisse decided not to let the whirlpool of fear take over and control her. She decided to break the shackles of her constitutional apprehension and seek help. Sydney decided not to wait for someone else to make the change and instead to be the one to make the change she wished to see in the world. Ethan, without a slightest hesitation, decided to choose family over his dream of Ph.D. Radha, though her heart sank into her boots, decided not to give up or run away when faced with a challenging situation and believed in herself. Kevin, without caving in into the captivating world of addictive forces, decided to be teetotaler and believed that there is still good in the world. At every major juncture in their life, they had different options to choose from, like what Audi had at her fifteenth birthday. When Audi's dad spoke to her those words of insight, she had two choices. She could have chosen to become wealthy, but she did not. The decision she made shaped her into what she is today. Fres and Mort also had two choices, but each of them made different decisions. I initially made a poor decision to marry Philip, but later I made a healthy decision to get back home.

People say we are the choices we make. But the last two days has taught me that it is neither true nor accurate. I think we are the decisions we make based on our ability to choose and decide from the choices that we have. Yes, **it's all about the decisions we make**.

Buddha is said to have attained enlightenment under a tree; I attained mine on Flight RN1729 en route to Chicago.

156

HOPE

All of a sudden the plane came to a complete stop. I was so deeply lost in my pensive thoughts that I didn't hear the pilot's announcements that we were landing, nor did I notice there was a crying baby in the aisle seat. It was around 8:30PM in Chicago and in about thirty minutes my kids would be sleeping. I hoped to be home to kiss them goodnight. I was confident that I would reach home in thirty minutes as I pre-booked an on-demand autonomous cab. I quickly started walking towards the pickup zone but I noticed something familiar in my peripheral vision. When I turned to see what it was, to my surprise, my daughter came running towards me, jumped and knocked me down to kiss me. My son was also super elated to see me and was trying to jump from the tight clutches of my mom. My whole family was there to greet me. As if their presence to receive me wasn't enough of an astonishment, as a second dose of surprise, they revealed that they bought an autonomous car during that weekend. Even more amazing was that my dad programmed our home address all by himself, though I had my suspicions that Laila helped him. With sparkling views of towering mountains of snow piled up off the road reminding us of the numbing cold wave that hit a few days ago, we reached home within thirty minutes.

My kids had already had dinner and all I had to do was to tuck them in bed. My parents had also eaten along with the kids, but they said that they do not mind having a light meal with me again after my shower. While I was in the bath, I was thinking of ways to thank my parents for taking care of my children while I was away. I realized being a parent is a relentless full-time job that starts right after conception and ends only with passing. A sacred job in which one deliberately takes up the responsibility to present a good human being to the world. I always had an argument that there can be bad people, but not bad parents. But my argument was proven erroneous after hearing Kevin's story. Though Kevin's mother played a significant negative role, which was supposed to adversely affect and undermine his life, his staunch and prudent decisions made him chose that he didn't want to be like his mom. Aided by his education and his virtuous character, though she was a bad parent, Kevin also realized that the true evil is not his mom and never loathed her. Then there is Ethan's mom, like Kevin's mom, also had a child at a very young age. Though she lost her husband at a young age, she didn't remarry as she was sure that she alone could provide enough love of two people and that Ethan would never miss not having a paternal figure. She became his best friend and they talked about everything. She made Ethan her world, her life's purpose, and didn't even entertain the idea of not remarrying as a sacrifice of her own happiness. Despite how their mothers were to them, both Kevin and Ethan are exemplary models for how men in today's world should be – the epitome of nobility.

Despite my arrogant behavior, I am lucky to have parents who stood beside me, aiding and cheering me on through thick and thin, but Fresco was not that lucky. Fres's parents ostracized and abandoned him when he needed them the most. They didn't want to be a part of his fresh beginning. Children need parents the most when they are at their lows. As a parent, our children should be our first priority and we should never abdicate our responsibilities especially when the child deserves a second chance.

Often parents assume that they know their children, but Mort proved that even parents don't know what and how their child is thinking. There is so much pressure built into our materialistic competitive world, parents are failing to realize how a child is dealing with the pressure. Only if Mort's parents had made conversations to understand what he really wanted to do, perhaps he would have had the courage to tell them about the assault. Mort was afraid of what his parents would say if they came to know about the incursion. Mort felt inferior and his self-confidence plummeted as a result of his parents constantly comparing him to others. Parents have to remember that every child is unique and special. Being different is not a failure. Everyone has their own specialty. If we all did the same, we would be bland clones of each other.

We need to inspire and motivate, not harass and force our children. Encouraging parents have a healthy relationship with their children like

Radha's mom, who involuntarily inspired her to become a chef, and supported her interests and her decision to pursue it as a career. But not all parents are in a position to help financially. Audi had a big family and they were just self-sufficient and self-sustaining with their basic needs. Her father didn't help her monetarily. The riches he gave his daughter were words of wisdom which helped her focus and become financially stable on her own. With one question, he made her question herself on the most valuable thing in life that makes any mountain of money worthless in comparison to it. He gave intangible capital to explore opportunities and stand on her own feet in immortal fame. He gave her priceless advice which she used to build an empire. Parents also need to identify the child's interest like what Abi's parents did. They noticed her fervor for fine arts and enrolled her in different art classes every summer which Abi relentlessly practiced and challenged every day.

No parent wants to raise a boorish child and no matter how much they tried to cultivate good practices, some parents end up being unfortunate to have an offspring who do not return gratitude, and I myself am the quintessential example of a mean child who couldn't appraise the value of parents, nor their love. So was Philip, who is a disgrace to his family's reputation. His parents were always cordial to me, and they even tried to put some sense into him to treat me as human. But Philip, in his arrogant irreverence towards his parents, brushed them away with his male chauvinism. As money and power had inebriated him to an inordinate extent, he was misguided into believing that beating and abusing a girl makes him masculine. On the other hand, Tanya's mom was careless and ignored Tanya's attitude. Her mom was an opportunist and divorced when Tanya was six years old. Since then she spent the alimony lavishly and in a way was responsible for Tanya's disposable and gold digger attitude.

We parents do have a major impact on our children than we think. Children mimic our actions, our attitude, and our body language. Childhood shapes the later life and parents are the children's first teachers. Most of the time what kids see is what they learn as if they are pre-wired to soak up everything and imitate. They may be deaf to advice, but they are always observing for their role model. We have to be parents only if we can happily accept the duty and never abrogate the lifetime parental responsibility of our children's character development. In addition, it is also true that we all have our own destinies. We can only show the children the right path. Whether they follow it or not, is a decision they have to make. But a few things that experience teaches us is that though we try to safeguard our little ones, there will be times where they have to learn the hard way, and we as parents should be mentally prepared for it. Just as too much or too little of anything is injurious, both exorbitant love and care towards the child, or extreme carelessness and comparison hinders self-confidence. I learned that parents should always love the child, rebuke when the child is wrong, and praise when the child makes an effort, but most importantly, do all of these while being supportive. In the end, we are all imperfect, assuming that there is a definite universal gold-standard definition for "perfection".

I failed to realize that criticism and judgment of my parents was motivated by their love for me. I also failed to realize that their remarks meant, "I love you so much and you are very precious to us." When my parents said they would not fund my college studies unless I started to study well, they actually wanted me to be strong, educated, knowledgeable, and independent. Rigidity and intransigence of our parents comes from their love for us, not hatred towards us. But somehow this concept gets lost in translation. When we were little kids and did not wash our hands before dinner, our parents used to say in a gentle, affable, loving voice, "Can you please go wash your hands before eating?" But when we start to grow up into our teenage years, the tone starts to change, and if we still do not wash our hands, then that same message changes to "What's wrong with you? How many times do I have to tell you to wash your hands before dinner? Are you insane, deranged, and demented? That's it. No dinner for you!" in rage. But in fact what the parents were trying to say is, "I love you very much and I want you to be safe and healthy. So, can you please wash your hands before eating?" Over the years, the love changes to displeasure and resentment, and all we perceive is their ire. Of course, parents too have to share some of the blame and are culpable to some extent.

As I stepped out of the shower, I vowed to not to lose my temper and always express myself in the language of 'love' in talks with my children. Not only that, I made an inviolable oath to always build their self-esteem and never to talk to them in a way that would hurt their confidence and morale. I vowed to see my children not as what they are, but what they can be. I promised to constantly encourage their efforts while establishing a good rapport with them to build an ecstatic family culture.

I joined the dinner table and told my parents everything that happened over the past few days. I later bid them good night and retreated to my room.

Of course a cluttered home is a sign of a living and breathing family, but my children went to so much extreme in two days that I started experiencing some exciting discoveries in my messy room. I was sure my parents tried their best, but they definitely couldn't keep up with their littering. As I started to clean up the clutter, I kept thinking about the enlightenment I had in the flight- that **it's all about the decisions** we make. When I started to unravel the intricacies of how we make unfamiliar decisions, which is entirely in our own control, I realized that while our ability to understand the problem, the situation, the available choices, and our thinking is based on our *knowledge*, judging the merits of available choices, selection and decision making is dependent on our *wisdom*. Though knowledge and wisdom may sound alike, or appear to be nuances, they are in fact vastly different. Knowledge can be gained from true education and it helps to comprehend the problem and understand the choices. Wisdom, on the other hand, is the ability to foresee the consequences of each choice and make a sensible decision. I guess the real-life story of Alfred Nobel makes a best example to fathom the difference between the two. Alfred Nobel, in his thirst for knowledge, invented dynamite, a powerful explosive. But in that pursuit, he failed to foresee that his invention will be used to kill more people faster than ever before.

Undoubtedly and undeniably, our competence in making the right decisions is limited by both our knowledge and wisdom. Our destiny is therefore decided by the wise decisions we make from the available choices. Though the deliberate selection from the available choices is just a matter of one step towards our destiny, clearly what matters is the direction of that step accompanied by whole-hearted implementation to unlock the door to life-changing personal transformation. In our life, at any point of time, we'll always see some good moments and some bad ones, some small events and some big. And as we introspect by quickly cruising through the myriad of decisions we have made, some of our conclusions appear to be the result of impulsive split-second emotional decisions and others the result of well-marinated reasoning. But in fact, the decisions we make are the product of conscious reasoning (logical thoughts) and intuitive feelings (emotions). It is completely up to us how much of rational reasoning versus visceral emotion comprises our decisions. But one major thing to keep in mind is, sometimes our decisions alone are not the basis for the outcome. Even some of our wisest decisions may result in bad consequences because the results depend not only on our decisions, but also on other people's decisions of which we lack any control. In other words, we are not entirely unaccountable but at the same time we are not always in complete control. While some of our decisions are risk-based, other decisions are based on our experience and wisdom. And the more experience is under our belt, the more options we see for the problem and we make a wiser decision.

The time was about 10:30PM and I couldn't sleep. As I quietly organized my room and individually stuck the magnetic alphabets my kids had thrown everywhere back on to the easel, I unconsciously combined the letters into the names of people I met, or those I consciously ruminated over the past few days.

ALEX
ABIGAIL
FRESCO
KEVIN
RADHA
ETHAN
MALCOLM
AUDRIANNA
SYDNEY
PHILIP
MORT
TANYA
CLARISSE

To my surprise, I saw the words "LIFE DECISIONS" hidden in it, analogous to a word search puzzle.

Each one of my friends' success was no accident, but what made them successful? With a firm conviction that I could uncover the recipe for success, I kept scrutinizing the lessons I learned during my interaction with diverse people. Every one of them came from different walks of life, with different ambitions, desires, aspirations, dreams, objectives, passions and goals. But the common thread I noticed among them is: optimism, diligence, dedication, commitment and perseverance - the qualities that cannot be bought, but can only be grown from within. They demonstrated that no matter how hard the goal, the longer one endures and persists with discipline, the more likely one will triumph, and success will ultimately follow. And if the person is emotionally connected to their ambitions and goals, they will be passionately committed to it because necessity is also the mother of success. Sometimes there is no career path already laid out to follow, no footsteps to walk in. It is like exploring an uncharted territory. Not everyone will see their whole path on the very first day. But we don't need to see the whole path, just the first step in the right direction is adequate to take the leap of faith. And those who take that leap of faith, those who commit to their goal even in the face of unforeseen obstacles, those who risk everything in pursuit of their goal and refuses to give up when confronted with impediments and hindrances, those who endures the pain in the face of insurmountable obstacles and perseveres, only they will prevail. Simply put: create a goal, believe in yourself and attack it as your life's purpose.

Similar to Darwinism, the Law of Success could be summed up in three virtues - patience, hard work, persistence. Anything valuable is the outcome of amalgamation of time, devoted dedicated effort, and perseverance. There doesn't exist a success without laborious effort. There is also no such thing as overnight triumph. Similar to knowledge and skills, achievements take time. One might lose because of bad luck, but one will never taste victory because of good luck, though in our foolishness we sometimes attribute a person's success to being lucky or gifted. We begin to sample success only when we start making wise decisions. While triumphs are the rewards of experimentation and our persistent drudgery, one also needs patience; the patience of a man trying to empty an ocean with a cup. One needs the patience of Michelangelo, a virtuoso craftsman venerated as one of the greatest artists of all time, who spent day after day, every day, for four years lying on his back, painting the ceiling of Sistine Chapel. One needs the persistence of Mahatma Gandhi and Martin Luther King Jr., who spent decades working to efface racism and prejudice from the face of Earth while serving several jail terms. One needs the endurance of medical researchers who often spend more than a decade to develop and test vaccines, often going back to square one.

As I was delving the formula for success, I noticed that the only thing my kids didn't touch is the 1300 pieces jigsaw puzzle I was working on before leaving for my interview. It made me think and realize that life is a jigsaw puzzle. To finish it, we have to put each piece right in its place. The puzzle pieces are the decisions that we have to make every day. Like few puzzle pieces, though they look the same, they can only fit in the right spot. Similarly, sometimes the decisions we make may look correct initially, but later we realize that it is not the right decision. And just as we can always replace the wrong puzzle pieces with the right ones, we can always replace the wrong decisions with the right ones. The puzzle is incomplete until we find the correct missing pieces. So is life. It is incomplete until we make the hard and right decisions.

A thought then occurred to me that I have two choices. Either I can wait for the offer letter from **SYMBIOSIS**, or I can try to make new opportunities within my current company. I felt that my career was stagnated in my current position, but was I simply confused the stability with stagnation? Because, rather than passively waiting for opportunities, if I put my mind to it, there is no doubt that I can actively find new opportunities to grow in my current company. And with my work ethic, I can make myself indispensable. Yet, the position at **SYMBIOSIS** is a better paying position. I could raise my kids well and take good care of my parents. Though it is true that I would get a hike in my salary, it wasn't that I was not currently content. Money enhances the quality of life but does not create happiness. My children, my parents and I were all happy here with what we had. It was then a quote I read a very long time ago popped into my head - "If you are willing to do more than you are paid to do, eventually you will be paid more than you do". So, irrespective of if I receive the offer letter or not, I decided to see every day, every experience, and every encounter as an opportunity to learn and a seed for growth. Just as there is beauty in everything fashioned by nature, everyday actually teaches us something. All we have to do is be willing to learn. In fact, we can learn a serious lesson even from a petty situation.

One such I learned was regarding winning the challenges in life. From Ethan's duel with Abi on Friday night, I learned that a winner is not the one who wins every challenge, but the one who willingly competes and fights till the end without giving up. I knew it would be very difficult to win any verbal or intellectual fights with Abi, and as a result I never initiated or participated in any debates with her. Ethan also knew it well that he cannot win against his adversary, a redoubtable debater.

However, Ethan still went ahead because he knew that the one who plays till the end and yet loses is still equivalent to a winner; but the wimp who fears and gives up at the beginning or aborts in the middle of the race is tantamount to a coward. I failed to realize that there is no chance of winning a race without competing. A loser is certainly not the one without a medal, but is definitely the one without a will to make an attempt or take the risk.

The clock displayed almost 11PM and I was ready to go to sleep to start a new day with a new me. I was now confident that I can make best use of any opportunity and equally confident that I don't have to wait for the opportunity. I can create an opportunity for myself. Almost everyone I met during the two days of reunion has written a page for themselves in the history. My friends made prudent decisions that made them what they are today. It is either through words of wisdom or by emotional tragedy that some people realize early on in their life, some others in their adulthood, some on their deathbed, and a lot more never in their lifetime that their life has amounted to nothing but consuming food and producing refuse. Upon this self-examination and realization, one changes, and almost everyone I met during those two days was past this awakening and doing their part to make this world a much better place to live. They were striving towards a life worth chronicling. How can I help? How can I create a colorful page for myself? How can I make a contribution to enrich someone's life? How can I help others through my experiences? What is the one thing that I love to do and where I can focus my energy while taking care of my health and having a healthy family time?

When we think of a change or improvement in our lives, we often think of external changes rather than internal changes, like the changes in our habits and thinking. The same is true for an opportunity. We often look for an opportunity to present to us and fail to create or realize that an opportunity is staring right at us. The wisdom of a person lies not in finding an opportunity but recognizing something that seems inconspicuous as an opportunity. I saw a tremendous opportunity right before me to create a bright and colorful page for myself in the annals of history. I saw two choices. I can either share the wisdom I gained from my experiences and encounters, or keep it only with me. Certainly, there was no need to deliberate on the choices for a long time. Fashioned from all the lessons my friends taught me, and what my own experiences taught me all these years, I, Alex Hope, will write a book that is worth reading and how it boils down to the fact that our life is the result of the decisions we make. Yes, that is what I will do. I will write a book that will help enrich people's lives and hopefully someone can someday attribute their turning point to my book.

But first, I need to clearly define a goal. A goal that is reasonable and realistic? No. Sensible goals only settle for ordinary. Audi's ambitions were impossible and so she became extraordinary. Though positive thinking and hard work with devotion will achieve almost anything, they are worthless if we don't dream big. The more unrealistic and impossible the dream or vision is, the more passion we would go after it. History has also shown us that the crazy ones who had crazy ideas and crazy enough to think that they can do it are the ones that made crazy impossible products. As Albert Einstein once said, "If at first the idea is not absurd, then there is no hope for it." However, there is still a need for caution and exercise of control because once we are committed to a goal in our mind, we do it no matter what it takes and even justify the decisions in our minds because an ambitious person will do anything to achieve their goals, including embracing unethical practices if needed.

I will make it my goal to publish a book in twenty-four months. But just as education without morality is useless, a goal without an action and persistence is dead. Though the neurology of every human is the same, the tiny ability to take an effective action is in fact the consequential difference between a successful person and an average but talented person. Really nothing happens until we release our inhibitions and take an action. And it is no small encouragement or push that my friends awarded me involuntarily. Instead of deferring until tomorrow, I will start writing my book right away, even if it means that I will have only the outline written before I go to sleep.

No wonder why Fres and Clarisse/Kevin have a predilection for video podcasts, and Ethan to teach students. A teacher, unfortunately underrated, affects eternity, and is one of the most unselfish and giving person who devotes themselves for the betterment of others. Teaching, a supreme art, is a vocation in which one person alone can make a boundless difference. A teacher instills everything they know to the student without expecting anything in return. And the wonderful thing is, everyone is capable of teaching something. I felt the responsibility of sharing my insights and it would be very selfish of me if I do not help others benefit from my priceless wealth of practical wisdom. I hope my book will help people to learn from my mistakes, to overcome fears that are impeding their growth, and will inspire young minds to choose the correct path and be better people to help our world to be a better place to live. And I also hope those who read my book, will then share, refer and encourage others to read it.

* * *

It took me two days of uninterrupted reading to finish the book. It was August 30, 2036, and I was about to start my freshman year in high school when my grandma gave me the book to read. My mom was away on a speaking engagement. As it was only a week away, covert operations were well underway for my super mom's surprise 40th birthday party. For my part, I decided to make a collage and a short movie from all the previous birthday pictures and videos. As I started to dig them out, I noticed that they jumped from seventeen to twenty-third birthday, and she looked completely different thereafter. I inquired about the missing pictures, but my grandma ignored me initially. As I kept pestering her, she handed me a book to read. It was my mom's memoir, but was mostly dominated by three days in December 2029 that changed the course of her life.

People only know my mom as a renowned inspirational and keynote speaker, but no one knows what made her become one as her memoir was never published. Neither do people know that she almost failed before she became a distinguished educator and a widely sought-after speaker for graduation ceremonies. Following that turning point in December 2029, with a fervent passion and taking it as a calling, she put her heart in and finished writing and editing the "Decisions" manuscript in nine months' time. But even after attending several writers' conferences, with no author platform or fan base, she failed to captivate the interest of a literary agent to land a book deal. Dozens of editors and independent publishers also rejected her work. Trying in vain for more than a year, which sorely tested her resolve to never surrender, she decided to self-publish.

As a self-help book written by an unknown author in the field, and with minimal marketing reach, the book hardly sold any. She barely broke-even with all the publishing costs, but I can still recollect that we had a big family success celebration as my mom accomplished her goal of publishing within two years of its conception.

Though the copies of her success recipe book were leaving the retailers shelf well below a sloth's pace, she didn't rest or lose hope in her work. I was almost 11 years old then. Just when I naively thought my mom was losing hope, the domino effect had begun in Texas. A high school principal who bought a copy of the book for her unruly teenage son, saw a huge potential and invited my mom to speak before the students. And very soon, my mom received a series of motivational public speaking requests from high schools, colleges, domestic violence shelters and even prisons to recount anecdotes of the life stories she learned to uplift, motivate, and instill a never give up attitude and never accept defeat mindset. Eventually her book outsold many that were on multiple bestseller lists.

What started off as a fun birthday planning has turned into an emotional journey for me knowing what she went through to give us a beautiful life. As it will only remind a past she's worked to move beyond, I ditched the idea of a picture collage and following our family tradition, I decided to write a compliment. A compliment for her efforts, for teaching me the value of family and friends, for showing me the fruits of patience and perseverance, for instilling the priceless value of morality, for training me to learn from mistakes, for developing my mindset that it is okay to fail but to never give up, for the skills to identify wrong influences in life, for the optimism of our last name, and above all, making me realize early in my life that life in general doesn't owe us anything to handout something; that instead of running away, we have to fight and work to get whatever we want.

I entitled my compliment, "*My mom, my hero.*" And I humbly signed my name: Laila Hope.

ABOUT THE AUTHORS

Sharat Srinivasula supports biomedical research at the National Institutes of Health in the understanding of HIV pathogenesis. With educational background in Mathematics and his multi-disciplinary work, he is an author and co-author on several biomedical publications. When he is not consciously designing experiments, one can find him cooking, reading, gardening and spending time with his two children.

Poornima Mynampati supports platforms team at Google in the role of a Thermal Engineer. With educational background in Thermal Engineering, she holds a patent in the cooling of data centers. When she is not consciously solving the overheating issues or providing optimal cooling solutions for data centers, one can find her baking, DIYing on home projects and playing with her daughter.

Both authors were born and brought up in India, but have been US residents for over ten years. This is the debut book for both authors. Though writing a book was never on their bucket list, a singular idea followed by a firm decision to act on it threw them into the world of writer's market.

ACKNOWLEDGMENTS

From the unfathomable depths of our hearts, we thank our respective spouses, **Sandhya Mynampati** and **Kartheek Vakicherla**, for their constant and never-ending support, encouragement, invaluable insight, feedback, and suggestions for improvement. We also fervently thank **Mridula Radha Srinivasula** for painstakingly typing and organizing the most frequent SAT/GRE words.

We thankfully acknowledge **Osei B. Simon** for critical reading of initial drafts of the manuscript and providing his comments and invaluable suggestions for improvement.

It is not a book if it didn't pass the dragonfly eyes of an able editor. In this regard, we are eternally grateful to our courteous and deft editor, **Ashleigh Marie Brown**, for providing constructive feedback and her services in editing while maintaining author's voice and style. No load of kudos can satisfactorily justify her judicious editing as we plead guilty of constraining her not to dispose of any of the 1200 SAT/GRE words while polishing our crude work.

A NOTE OF GRATITUDE TO THE READER

We, the authors, express our sincere gratitude to you for deciding to read "**It's all about the decisions we make**" from millions of other books out there. We hope this book will add or has already added value to your daily life. If this book benefited you, please share it with your family, friends and colleagues, and follow us on Facebook (@poornima.sharat.ms) for more information and discussion about the book.

As you are already aware, most people make their decision to read a specific book based on the reviews. In addition, we find ample nourishment and compensation though your encouraging feedback and reviews. *Inspire us by posting a review on Amazon.*

We would also like to hear from you directly. You can reach us easily through email: poornima.sharat.ms@gmail.com

APPENDIX

abase
abate
abdicate
aberration
abet
abhor
abide
abject
abjure
abnegation
abort
abridge
abrogate
abscond
absolution
abstain
abstemious
abstract
abstruse
abyss
accede
accentuate
accessible
acclaim
accolade
accommodating
accord
accost
accretion
acerbic
acquiesce
acquire
acrimony
acumen
acute
adamant
adept
adhere
admonish

adorn
adroit
adulation
adulterate
adumbrate
adversary
adverse
advocate
aerial
aesthetic
affable
affinity
affluent
affront
aggrandize
aggregate
aggrieved
agile
agriculture
aisle
alacrity
alias
allay
allege
alleviate
allocate
aloof
altercation
amalgamate
amateur
ambiguous
ambivalent
ameliorate
amenable
amenity
amiable
amicable
amorous
amorphous
anachronistic

analgesic
analogous
anathema
anecdote
anesthesia
anguish
animated
annex
annul
anomaly
anonymous
antagonize
antecedent
antediluvian
anthology
anthropology
antipathy
antiquated
antiseptic
antithesis
anxiety
apathetic
aplomb
apocryphal
appalling
appease
appraise
apprehend
approbation
apt
aquatic
arable
arbiter
arbitrary
arbitration
arboreal
arcane
archaeological
archaic
archetypal

ardor
arduous
arid
arrogant
articulate
artifact
artisan
ascertain
ascetic
ascribe
aspersion
aspirations
aspire
assail
assert
assess
assiduous
assuage
astute
asylum
atone
atrophy
attain
attribute
atypical
audacious
audible
augment
auspicious
austere
authoritative
autonomous
avarice
avenge
aversion
avert
avid
awestruck

baffle
balk
ballad
banal
bane
bard
bashful
battery
befuddle
beguile
behemoth
belie
benevolent
benign
berate
bereft
beseech
bewilder
bias
blandish
blemish
blight
boisterous
bolster
bombastic
boon
boorish
bourgeois
brazen
brusque
buffet
burnish
buttress
burgeon

Cacophony
cadence
cajole

calamity
calibrate
callous
calumny
camaraderie
candid
candor
canny
cantankerous
canvas
capacious
capacity
capitulate
capricious
captivate
caricature
carouse
catalog
catalyst
catalyze
catastrophic
caucus
caustic
censure
cerebral
chaos
charlatan
chastise
chauvinist
cherish
chicanery
chide
choreography
chronicle
chronological
circuitous
circumlocution
circumscribed
circumvent
clairvoyant

clamor
clandestine
clarity
clemency
cloying
coagulate
coalesce
cobbler
coerce
cogent
cognizant
coherent
collaboration
collateral
colloquial
colossal
combustion
commemorate
commend
commendation
commensurate
commodious
compelling
compendium
compensate
complacency
complement
compliant
compliment
compound
comprehensive
compress
compunction
concede
conciliatory
concise
concoct
concomitant
concord
condemn

condescending
condolence
condone
conducive
conduit
confection
confidant
conflagration
confluence
conformist
conformity
congeal
congenial
congregation
congruity
connive
connoisseur
conscientious
consensus
consequential
consolation
console
consonant
conspicuous
constituent
constrain
construe
consummate
consumption
contemporaneous
content
contentious
contravene
contrite
contusion
conundrum
convene
convention
convivial
convoluted

copious
cordial
coronation
corroborate
corrosive
cosmopolitan
counteract
coup
covert
covet
crafty
craven
credulity
crescendo
criteria
culmination
culpable
cultivate
cumulative
cunning
cupidity
curative
cursory
curt
curtail
cynical

daunting
dearth
debacle
debase
debauch
debilitate
debunk
decisive
decorous
decry
deface
defamatory

defer
deference
deferential
defile
deft
defunct
delegate
deleterious
deliberate
delineate
demagogue
demarcation
demean
demeanor
demure
denigrate
denounce
depict
deplore
depravity
deprecate
derelict
deride
derivative
desiccated
desolate
despondent
despot
destitute
desultory
deter
devious
devoid
dialect
diaphanous
diatribe
dichotomy
didactic
differentiate
diffident

diffuse
digress
dilate
dilettante
diligent
diminish
diminutive
diplomatic
dirge
disaffected
disavow
discern
disclose
discord
discordant
discredit
discreet
discrepancy
discretion
discursive
disdain
disgruntled
disheartened
disparage
disparate
dispatch
dispel
disperse
dispute
disregard
dissemble
disseminate
dissent
dissipate
dissonance
dissuade
dither
diverge
divert
divine

divulge
docile
doctrine
dogmatic
domestic
dormant
dour
dubious
dupe
duplicity
duress
dynamic

earnest
ebullient
eccentric
eclectic
ecstatic
edict
efface
effervescent
efficacious
effrontery
effulgent
effusive
egotist
egregious
elaborate
elated
elegy
elicit
elite
eloquent
elucidate
elude
emaciated
embellish
embezzle
embroiled

emend
eminent
emollient
emote
empathy
emphatic
empirical
emulate
enamor
encompassed
encore
encumber
endemic
endure
enervate
engender
enigma
enigmatic
enmity
ennui
entail
enthrall
ephemeral
epitome
equanimity
equivocal
eradicate
erroneous
erudite
eschew
esoteric
espouse
esteemed
estrange
ethereal
etymology
eulogy
euphony
euphoric
evanescent

evince
evoke
exacerbate
exalt
exasperate
excavate
exculpate
excursion
execrable
exemplary
exhort
exigent
exonerate
exorbitant
expedient
expiate
explicit
exploit
expunge
extant
extol
extraneous
extravagant
extricate
exuberant
exult

fabricated
facade
facile
facilitate
fallacious
fallible
fastidious
fathom
fatuous
feasible
fecund
felicitous

feral
fervent
fetid
fetter
fickle
fidelity
figurative
flabbergasted
flaccid
flagrant
fledgling
flippant
florid
flourish
flout
foil
foment
forage
forbearance
forestall
forlorn
forsake
fortify
fortitude
fortuitous
forum
foster
fractious
fraught
frenetic
frivolous
frugal
fundamental
furtive
futile

garish
garrulous
gauche

generalization

genial

germane

glutton

goad

gourmand

grandiloquence

grandiose

gratuitous

gregarious

grievous

guile

gullible

hackneyed

hapless

harangue

hardy

harrowing

haughty

hedonism

hedonist

heinous

heterogeneous

hiatus

hierarchy

homogeneous

hostile

humble

humility

hypocrisy

hypothetical

iconoclast

ideologies

idiosyncratic

idolatrous

ignominious

illicit

illuminate

illusory

immaculate

immerse

immodest

immutable

impeccable

impecunious

imperative

imperceptible

imperious

impertinent

imperturbable

impervious

impetuous

implacable

implausible

implement

implicit

impregnable

improvise

impudent

impute

inane

inarticulate

incarnate

incendiary

incessant

inchoate

incisive

inclination

incongruity

inconsolable

inconspicuous

incontrovertible

incorrigible

incredulous

increment

incumbent

indefatigable

indictment

indifferent

indigenous

indigent

indignant

indolent

indomitable

induce

indulge

ineffable

inept

inexorable

inextricable

infamy

infusion

ingenious

inhibit

inimical

iniquity

innate

innocuous

innovate

innovative

innuendo

inoculate

inquisitive

insatiable

insidious

insinuate

insipid

insolent

instigate

integral

intemperate

interject

interminable

interrogate

intimate

intransigent

intrepid
intuitive
inundate
inure
invective
inveterate
invigorate
inviolable
invoke
irascible
iridescent
irreverence
irrevocable

jaded
jubilant
judicious
juxtapose

knell
kudos

laceration
laconic
lament
languid
larceny
largesse
lassitude
latent
laudatory
lavish
legerdemain
legitimate
lenient
lethargic
levee

liability
liberated
libertarian
licentious
limpid
linchpin
lithe
litigant
longevity
loquacious
lucid
luminous
lurid

maelstrom
magnanimous
malediction
malevolent
malice
malinger
malleable
mandate
manifest
manifold
mar
maudlin
maverick
mawkish
maxim
meager
mendacious
mediocre
medley
melodrama
mercurial
meritorious
metamorphosis
meticulous
mimic

misanthrope
mitigate
moderate
modest
mollify
monarch
monotony
morass
mores
morose
multifarious
mundane
munificence
mutable
myriad

nadir
naive
nascent
nebulous
nefarious
negligent
neophyte
nocturnal
noisome
nomadic
nominal
nonchalant
nondescript
nostalgia
notorious
novice
noxious
nuance
nurture

obdurate
oblique

oblivious
obscure
obsequious
obsolete
obstinate
obviate
occlude
odious
ominous
omniscient
onerous
opaque
opportune
oppress
opulent
oration
ornamentation
ornate
orthodox
oscillate
ostensible
ostentatious
ostracize
overwhelming

pacify
painstaking
palatable
palette
palliate
pallid
panacea
paradigm
paradox
paragon
paramount
parasite
pariah
parody

parsimony
partisan
patent
pathology
pathos
patronizing
paucity
pejorative
pellucid
penchant
penitent
penultimate
penurious
perennial
perfidious
perfunctory
periphery
permeate
pernicious
perpetuate
perplex
perspicacity
pertinacious
perusal
pervasive
petty
petulance
phenomenon
philanthropic
phlegmatic
pillage
pinnacle
piqued
pithy
pittance
placate
placid
plastic
platitude
plaudits

plausible
plenitude
plethora
pliable
plummet
poignant
polemic
popularize
portent
potable
pragmatic
precarious
precedent
precipitous
preclude
precocious
predilection
preponderance
prepossessing
presage
prescient
prescribe
presumption
presumptuous
pretense
prevaricate
primeval
pristine
privation
probity
proclivity
prodigal
profane
profligate
profound
profuse
prohibitive
proliferate
prolific
prolong

prominent
promulgate
propaganda
propagate
propensity
prophetic
propitious
propriety
prosaic
proscribe
protean
provocative
prowess
prudent
prurient
puerile
pugnacious
pulchritude
punctilious
pungent
punitive
putrid

quagmire
quaint
quandary
quantitative
quell
querulous
quibble
quiescent
quixotic
quotidian

rail
rancid
rancor
rapport

rash
raucous
raze
rebuke
rebut
recalcitrant
recant
recapitulate
reciprocate
reclusive
reconcile
rectitude
redoubtable
redundant
refract
refurbish
refute
regurgitate
reiterate
relegate
relish
remedial
reminiscence
remiss
remorse
renovate
renown
renounce
repentant
replete
repose
reprehensible
reprieve
reproach
reprobate
reprove
repudiate
repugnant
repulse
reputable

requisition
rescind
reservoir
resilient
resolute
resolution
resolve
respite
resplendent
restitution
restive
reticent
retract
revel
revere
revoke
rhapsodize
rhetoric
rife
rigorous
ruminate

Saccharine
sacrosanct
sagacity
salient
salutation
salve
sanctimonious
sanction
sanguine
sarcasm
satiate
satire
scarce
scathing
scintillating
scorn
scrupulous

scrutinize
scurrilous
sedentary
seminal
sensual
sentimental
serendipity
serene
simultaneous
sinuous
skeptical
smug
sobriety
solemn
solicitous
soluble
solvent
somber
somnolent
sophomoric
soporific
sovereign
sparse
specious
spectrum
speculative
spontaneous
spurious
stagnate
staid
stifled
stigma
stingy
stoic
stolid
strenuous
strident
stupefy
subjective
subjugate

sublime
submissive
subpoena
subsequent
substantiate
subtle
succinct
superficial
superfluous
supplant
suppress
surfeit
surmise
surreptitious
surrogate
susceptible
swarthy
sycophant

tacit
taciturn
tact
tactile
tangential
tantamount
tedious
temerity
temperate
tenable
tenacious
tenuous
terrestrial
therapeutic
thwart
timorous
tirade
toady
tome
torpid

torrid
tortuous
tractable
tranquil
transcend
transgress
transient
transmute
travesty
treacherous
tremulous
trenchant
trepidation
trite
trivial
truculent
truncate
turgid
turmoil
turpitude
tyranny

ubiquitous
umbrage
uncanny
unctuous
undermine
underscore
undulate
untenable
upbraid
usurp
utilitarian
utopia

vacillate
vacuous
validate

vapid
variegated
vehemently
veneer
venerated
veracity
verbose
verdant
vestige
vex
vicarious
vicissitude
vigilant
vigor
vilify
vindicated
vindictive
virtuoso
viscous
vitriolic
vituperate
vivacious
vocation
vociferous
vulgar
vulnerable
volatile

Wallow
wane
wanton
warrant
wary
weary
whimsical
wily
winsome
wistful
wizened

wrath
waver

Yoke

Zealous
zenith
zephyr

Made in the USA
Las Vegas, NV
01 September 2021